hell House

& OTHER TRUE HAUNTINGS FROM AROUND THE WORLD

Alison Rattle and Allison Vale

BARNES
&NOBLE

NEW YORK

© 2005 Gusto Company AS

Written by Alison Rattle and Allison Vale
Illustrations and Photography: Getty Images and Corbis Images
Executive Editor and original concept: James Tavendale
Edited by Katherine Robinson and Ewan Carpenter
Designed by Jeffrey Swartz

Published exclusively for Barnes & Noble, Inc., by Gusto Company

ISBN 0-7607-7221-5

Printed and bound in China

05 06 07 08 09 MP 9 8 7 6 5 4 3 2 1

Contents

Introduction

Have you always wanted to be a great storyteller, or do you just have a ghoulish desire to scare the living daylights out of the kids? This compendium of supernatural sightings will allow you to achieve both. It will take you on a round-the-world journey and alight at the most haunted locations on the planet. But luckily for you, you can read about them from the "ghost-free zone" of your own couch.

Whether you're a skeptic looking for proof or a believer steadily collating evidence, ghost stories are a constant source of fascination. In this book we'll convert the cynics and arm the enthusiasts with facts and figures, first-hand accounts of ghostly sightings, and the history behind the scenes.

Ghost stories are often rich in history, and it's the background that brings these stories to life. This book will set the scene and submerge you in a ghoulish underworld. From the murky depths of Medieval England to the brutal plains of contemporary Eastern Europe, you'll experience the unearthly presences that wreak havoc to this day.

So board the ghost train. Buckle up for the ride of your life . . . and spare a thought for those whose lives are tormented by the specters that lurk within these pages.

Identifying Visitors from the Spirit World

G hosts appear in many different forms and have a variety of motives, attachments, and preoccupations, but they fall into distinctive categories. Before attempting to seek out ghosts and ghouls it is important to familiarize yourself with the various metaphysical substances you may encounter.

APPARITION: An apparition appears in human form, is sometimes transparent, and wears clothing of the period to which it belongs. It is notoriously difficult to capture on film. An apparition may be directly in front of you, but still fail to appear on a developed photograph. Apparitions are frequently associated with old houses, churches, theaters, castles, and cemeteries. There are also many reported cases of religious apparitions of saints and the faces of Jesus or the Virgin Mary. While many people claim to see apparitions to gain attention, the handful of genuine cases are often characterized by the modesty of witnesses who neither invite the visitation nor seek the public attention which it generates.

COLLECTIVE APPARITION: When more than one person witnesses a ghost or spirit phenomenon, independently or simultaneously, it is classed as a collective apparition. Nearly ten percent of reported cases of apparitions fall into this category, and once fraud has been ruled out, they are more likely to be genuine sightings.

ECTOPLASM: Commonly understood to be a substance secreted by spirits and exuded from mediums communicating with the spirit world, ectoplasm is now widely associated with a cloudy vaporous mist that may take the form of a human body. It has been captured photographically, and is seen to hover above the ground as a swirl of gray or white matter. It may linger in one place or travel fast and is usually spotted outdoors.

ELEMENTAL: An inhabitant of one of the four elements (fire, earth, air, and water). Elementals exist somewhere between the realm of the human and spirit worlds. They are often associated with forces of nature rather than the souls of the deceased, but they are nevertheless powerful metaphysical entities which sometimes inhabit the bodies of the living and possess them. Another definition of elementals is spirits which can change into solid matter and back again at will.

EVIL SPIRIT: A shape-shifting non-human spirit that usually appears after being summoned, either with a Ouija board or through satanic worship. It can appear as a monster or may disguise itself as a friendly spirit, but it is dangerous and seeks to harm and cause destruction.

GHOST LIGHTS: These have been sighted all over the world and in many cultures. They are mysterious lights, seen at a distance, usually appearing as blue or yellow spheres, which can appear to blink. Some reports liken them to a bobbing candle flame. This phenomenon is also known by its Latin name *ignis fatuus*, or "foolish flame," because anyone attempting to follow or catch one of these lights is thought to place himself or herself in mortal danger. Skeptics attribute it to swamp gas, magnetism, or electricity. Ghost lights have been reported for centuries and were once known as "will-'o-the-wisp," an omen of death representing the ghost of a sinner condemned to wander the earth forever.

GHOUL: A grotesque, flesh-eating demon that robs graves to satisfy its evil hunger for the recently buried. It has its origins in Arabic folklore and is best known today as the living dead, a reanimated corpse inhabited by evil spirits. Ghouls are rumored to live near graveyards and are nocturnal; some believe they are vampires that have degenerated into inarticulate and ravenous automatons, robbed of freewill, intelligent thought, or the ability to feel pain. They are commonly described as having long arms, sunken gray faces, bulging eyes, and sharp teeth and nails.

ORBS: Translucent spheres of light which hover above the ground and dart erratically through the air. Many believe that ghosts prefer to take on an orb shape, as it requires less energy than other apparitions.

They differ from ghost lights in that photographed ghost scenes show orbs as spherical lights (rather than a flickering flame), some with a nucleus, others transparent. If moving fast, a trail of light may appear to emanate from the sphere. The majority of orbs captured in photographs are probably caused by the camera's flash or weather conditions.

PHANTOM ANIMALS: Many corporeal ghosts take the form of animals rather than humans. It may be the benign spirit of a loved pet or faithful companion which appears to its master and is often seen performing a habitual act, such as lying in front of the fire or waiting by the front door. However, there are many sightings of strange and malevolent beasts such as ghostly black dogs, phantom birds, or horses.

POLTERGEISTS: Taken from the German words *poltern* (to knock) and *geist* (spirit), poltergeists are careless, destructive forces. They are most renowned for their domestic disturbances, such as moving or displacing objects within a home, sometimes with great speed and force. Other manifestations include foul language, frightening voices, knocks and bumps, noxious smells, pools of liquid, fire-starting, and writing on walls. Some may have physical expression and actually cause harm to an individual through physical contact.

They are most active at night and in the presence of humans who are classed as "agents" and act as a focus for paranormal activity. Recent research indicates that poltergeists actually emanate from the unconscious minds of humans. The disturbances may last only seconds or minutes but have also been documented to last from hours to several months.

POSSESSED OBJECTS: Inanimate objects that move, change appearance, or make noise. Sometimes an episode occurs while a person is watching, or they return to find that a disturbance has taken place while they were away. They include vehicles such as ghost ships or phantom trains heard bumping along tracks that were removed many years earlier. This phenomenon is often associated with the influence of a ghost that is emotionally attached to a place or object and may be showing anger or disapproval of how the present-day occupants or owners have changed it. Ghost vehicles are often linked to a fatal accident.

RESIDUAL HAUNTING: This is the playback of a past event, trapped in a continuous loop. It is often associated with past events involving great trauma and tragedy. A person is seen or heard performing a repetitive action—walking down a flight of stairs, crossing a garden, screaming in agony—at the same time or place and by many different independent witnesses. Researchers believe that it is possible for certain building materials to retain the energy of an event, and "record" it electromagnetically in a similar way to modern video or audio tape, and then replay the eerie fragment when the atmospheric conditions are right, or when a person who is especially sensitive to its bizarre energy passes by.

SHADOW GHOSTS: Easily confused with normal shadows, these dark ghostly apparitions are often spotted at a distance or in peripheral vision, and are between two and ten feet long. They are often experienced as a small darting essence in the corner of the eye, or as a larger and more menacing humanoid presence.

VORTEX: These swirling funnel-shaped masses of air or energy are believed by some to be portals between this world and the spirit realm that allow ghosts to transform into orbs. Also known as "funnel ghosts," they are often felt as a cold spot and are rarely seen outdoors.

WRAITH: Sometimes a person sees a loved one appear briefly to them, or hears their voice offering a warning or advice. The loved one needn't be a ghost; they are often alive and many miles away. In some cases these appearances coincide with the death of the loved one, or occur during a time of crisis for the witness.

Popular Questions Answered

WHAT ARE GHOSTS? Every culture holds beliefs in the concept of life after death. Reincarnation and ghosts are important codes of faith for many of them. However, in the Western world, ghosts are believed to be manifestations of the spirits of the deceased whose souls, for reasons unexplained, still exist on earth. Energy cannot be destroyed, only changed, and so if a person's energy is not extinguished by death, the person remains a force or an entity long after their bodily destruction.

Some believe that ghosts are telepathic images that are received and interpreted by those who have heightened sensitivity; others believe that a ghost sighting is the result of a time slip (Albert Einstein proved that time is non-linear, making this theoretically possible).

Another theory suggests that during incidents which involve high stress and trauma high amounts of energy and electrical impulses are generated, and an electromagnetic imprint lingers in the vicinity for a long time afterward.

ARE GHOSTS EVIL? While ghosts may be destructive, particularly polter-geists, many researchers reason that ghosts are not evil but merely restless spirits attempting communication with the living. Many ghost sightings can even be a pleasant experience, or if uncomfortable, at least non-threatening. It is rare for a ghost to inflict actual bodily harm; when this occurs it is usually in the form of scratches, bites, and bruises, which may lead skeptics to dismiss them as self-inflicted wounds. There have been reports of whole communities being terrorized by rapacious malevolent spirits called *incubi* and *succubi*, but these are mercifully rare.

WHERE HAVE THE MOST GHOSTS BEEN SIGHTED? Many countries stake their claim to being one of the most haunted locations in the world. It's good for tourism, and ghost stories abound in countries where community links are strong and there is a healthy openness to all things unexplained. Scotland and Ireland are contenders for the title of most haunted places in Europe, while every state in the United States has an abundance of hair-raising tales. However, in many Eastern cultures such as Thailand—where, for example, most large trees are said to house a spirit—ghosts are a natural part of everyday life.

WHEN ARE GHOSTS LIKELY TO APPEAR? Ghosts can appear anywhere and at any time, so it's more a question of "to whom" than when. Studies show that one in ten of us have the ability to see ghosts; children are more capable than adults, suggesting that adults lose the ability or somehow develop a blocking mechanism; women appear to be more ghost-savvy than men, and the higher a person's IQ, the lower their ghost-spotting potential. Those who try too hard to see ghosts will fail, since the most conducive mental state appears to be calm receptiveness.

WHY ARE GHOSTS EARTHBOUND ENTITIES? Many believe that ghosts are trapped in a human environment because they harbor negative energies—*e.g.*, a residual anger that grips them beyond the grave. It is not until they release these negative energies that they can finally be at peace and go to heaven—or hell. There is a common belief that some ghosts remain earthbound in order to protect those who were closest to them while living.

WHO ARE THE MOST FAMOUS GHOST HUNTERS? According to the writer Eric Russell, the golden age for ghost hunting was the years between the 1870s and the 1930s. Before then, ghost hunters were synonymous with spirit raisers and after that period the focus shifted to include UFOs.

Harry Price is one of the most influential and famous figures in the history of ghost hunting. Born in 1881, he was a flamboyant self-publicist who had no scientific training, which made him many enemies in the field of psychic research. However, he pioneered the scientific study of paranormal phenomena, and he was also very skilled at exposing hoaxes and fraudsters. One of these was "spirit photographer" William Hope who, until he encountered Price, had made a good living taking portraits which included deceased relatives. Price proved he was using double exposure to create these images. He also ended the careers of many so-called mediums.

Another giant in the field was Harry Houdini (1874-1926), who is better known for escapology than for his other passion—exposing mediums. He was fascinated with all things supernatural, and after his death thousands of fans and mediums attempted to contact his spirit. However, always the skeptic, Houdini had the last laugh. Before he died, he had agreed to a secret code word with his wife; curiously, none of those who claimed to have contacted the great showman mentioned it.

Nandor Fodor (1895-1964) is best known for his groundbreaking work with poltergeists. His most famous case was that of seventeen-year-old Ted Jones from Baltimore, Maryland, during which he invented the term "Recurrent Spontaneous Psychokinesis" to explain the way he believed the boy was able to channel psychokinetic energy subconsciously, and cause numerous terrifying poltergeist incidents.

The Ghost Club of London is the oldest group of ghost hunters in the world. Formed in 1862, it has attracted some of the most esteemed ghost hunters, and members including Charles Dickens, Sir Julian Huxley, Arthur Koestler, Dennis Wheatley, Sir Osbert Sitwell, and William Butler Yeats. It is still in existence today.

HOW DO YOU KNOW IF WHAT YOU'RE SEEING IS A GHOST? It is important to stay calm and rule out all other plausible explanations. If you are stressed or agitated, your judgment will be affected and cause you to interpret all manner of things with a supernatural bias. Think rationally; the knocking on the wall could be the air-conditioning or the water heating system; maybe that scratching sound is a bird nesting in the chimney. A good ghost hunter is a curious mixture of skeptic and believer, so keep an open mind but don't be carried away by your own fears or desires.

Here are a few things to bear in mind before you conclude you are in the presence of a ghost:

- Temperature changes cause building materials (especially wood and metal) to shrink and expand and may explain many of the moans and creaks in the attic.

- Weather is a major factor in making houses creak and groan. A spell of unusual weather (drought, flooding) will be followed by a settling period.

- New houses make noises, too. They need time to settle as the different components adjust.

- Rodents are more common than you might think. Many houses have mice scurrying behind the walls.

- Routine noises that happen at the same time everyday or night are likely to have an environmental cause—such as temperature or humidity changes.

Which locations are most likely to be haunted?

1. CEMETERIES: Some people believe that ghosts persist here because they are places where great emotional loss has been experienced, and it also encourages the living to contemplate death and the afterlife. That, and the large number of buried corpses, exert a powerful hold on wandering souls.

2. HOTELS: They are places that have witnessed a lot of joy and laughter, but also dramas and deaths; consequently every old hotel seems to have a haunted room and a ghost story which can be traced back to a direful event in its history.

3. PUBLIC HOUSES: When the alcohol is flowing, it is little wonder that judgment becomes blurred and the imagination more suggestible, so you might think it inevitable that pubs generate ghost stories. However, bear in mind that this is another hub of human activity and many a bar brawl has ended in tragedy.

4. MUSEUMS: Filled with artifacts, each with a colorful history, ghosts often have a strong attachment to objects, making a museum the ideal place to bump into a bevy of otherworldly beings.

5. BATTLEFIELDS: Human suffering and tragic loss on an apocalyptic scale make these sites powerful anchors for paranormal activity. The great battles of Europe and the American Civil War have generated hundreds of tales of supernatural occurrences.

6. CASTLES: Scheming, murderous nobles, feuding families, cruelly treated slaves and servants , despotism and death in the dungeons—castles are the backdrop which accommodate centuries of brutishness. They pay the price with their restless spirits.

7. DERELICT PRISONS: The prisons of past generations have witnessed unspeakable atrocities and the relentless erosion of the human will. Many innocents have been deprived of their liberty and haunt the sites of their injustice. These are prime sites for ghost hunting.

8. THEATERS: Actors have always been a superstitious bunch, but that alone cannot account for the high level of ghostly traffic within their place of work. Even where theaters have burned down, the ghosts return when they are rebuilt. Not only are these temples of heightened emotion, but they are notoriously dangerous, and many have lost their lives behind the scenes.

9. CROSSROADS: These are places of great spiritual power and have been linked with the spirit world since antiquity. Maybe it is because of the strange energy disruption that is caused where two roads cross and where choice has played a part in the destinies of countless travelers.

10. CRIME SCENES: When a person is murdered, the soul is ripped from the body abruptly before the person has had time to prepare for death. It sends out a network of grief as loved ones learn of the violation; residual hauntings abound here.

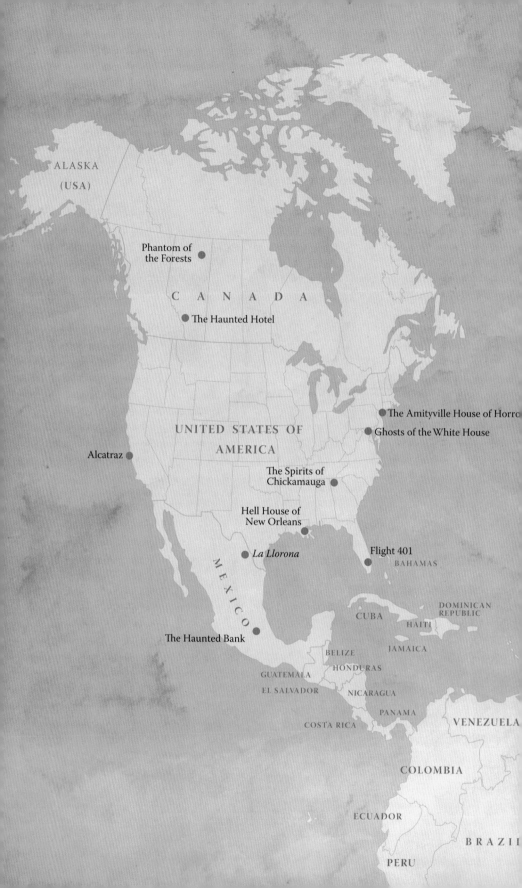

ALASKA
(USA)

Phantom of
the Forests ●

C A N A D A

● The Haunted Hotel

UNITED STATES OF

AMERICA

● The Amityville House of Horro

● Ghosts of the White House

Alcatraz ●

The Spirits of
Chickamauga ●

Hell House of
New Orleans

La Llorona ●

Flight 401 ●

BAHAMAS

M E X I C O

DOMINICAN
REPUBLIC

CUBA

HAITI

JAMAICA

The Haunted Bank ●

BELIZE

HONDURAS

GUATEMALA

EL SALVADOR

NICARAGUA

PANAMA

VENEZUELA

COSTA RICA

COLOMBIA

ECUADOR

B R A Z I L

PERU

North America

Across a continent where so many dreams have become a reality, the human suffering that lies beneath occasionally impinges on the personal triumphs. From the crushed spirits of Alcatraz to the wilds of Canada and the great Rio Bravo of Mexico, the resonance of human tragedies has resulted in some of the world's most enthralling hauntings.

Ghosts of the White House

I t is usually the case that sites most likely to be haunted are those that have witnessed great sorrows, tragedies, and loves. It is therefore no surprise to learn that the White House has its fair share of spectral residents. Its very name is linked to an act of violence, as its gray Virginia stone walls had to be painted white to cover scorch marks after it was set afire by British troops in the War of 1812.

The White House stands at 1600 Pennsylvania Avenue, Washington, D.C. It is also known as the executive mansion, having been home to nearly every president of the United States.

Building of the White House began in October 1792, when George Washington was president. He did not get the chance to live there, as work was not completed on the building until John Adams took office in 1800.

It is a grandiose building, and the only private, head-of-state home to be open to the public free of charge. With its six residence levels, 134 rooms, three elevators, movie theater, and bowling alley, it is the most popular tourist attraction in America. Indeed, many of its former residents must have enjoyed its charms so much that they refused ever to leave.

The most prominent spirit of the White House is that of Abraham Lincoln, sixteenth president of the United States. His administrations saw much violence; indeed, his election to office in 1860 incited the disunion of the Southern states, which led to the Civil War from 1861 to 1865. His life ended

tragically in April 1865 when he was assassinated by Southern sympathizer John Wilkes Booth.

After Lincoln's death, his footsteps were often heard by members of the White House staff, pacing to and fro on the second floor. His ghostly apparition was first observed during Calvin Coolidge's administration (1923–1929). First Lady Grace Coolidge saw Lincoln standing in the Oval Office gazing out of a window overlooking the Potomac River. He has been seen many times since in the same contemplative pose—thinking what, we do not know. President Nixon is purported to have taken advice from the wise old spirit of "Honest Abe."

Lincoln's ghost is reported to knock on bedroom doors late at night, startling guests awake and materializing just long enough to ensure them a wakeful and terrified night. He often appears at a time of national crisis, stomping heavily along floors and rapping impatiently on doors. A bodyguard working under President Benjamin Harrison once attended a séance to plead with Abraham to stop his nightly capers and allow him enough sleep to carry out his work of protecting the president. A more endearing sighting was that of Abraham sitting on the edge of a bed in the Lincoln bedroom, pulling on his boots.

In life, Abraham and his wife, Mary, were very spiritual people who often sought the guidance of mediums, particularly following the death of Abraham's favorite son, Willie. Abraham never recovered from the death of his beloved little boy and was often heard talking softly to him while alone in his office. Perhaps this great sadness is what causes his spirit to linger, or maybe it was the suddenness of his own death, which caused him to leave behind unfinished business. Lincoln had several premonitions concerning his own death, one occurring just two days before the assassination.

The oldest known ghost of the White House is that of former First Lady Abigail Adams. She and her husband, President John Adams, were the first occupants of the house. Despite its luxuries, the heating was wholly inadequate, and washing had to be dried in the East Room of the residence. To this day Abigail Adams can be seen gliding toward the East Room, her arms full of transparent washing as she disappears through the door.

Other lesser known hauntings include that of former President Andrew Jackson, whose ghostly laughter can still be heard in the Rose Room where he liked to sleep, and apparently still does. Mary Todd Lincoln claimed to have heard his rantings and heavy footsteps on numerous occasions.

It is said that in the Rose Room and the Yellow Oval Room a ghostly voice proclaims, "I am Mr. Burns." This has to be the declaration of David Burns, the man who gave the government the land on which the White House is built. He obviously feels his generous donation has not been sufficiently acknowledged.

The grounds of the White House are haunted by the indignant spirit of Dolley Madison. Wife of the fourth president, James Madison, she was responsible for the planting of the delightful rose garden. When Woodrow Wilson took office in 1912, his wife decided the rose garden needed replanting. Before the plan could be carried out, the ghost of Dolley Madison appeared to the terrified garden staff and demanded they leave her precious roses well alone. The alarmed gardeners were so intimidated that they refused to touch any of the roses. Dolley's garden has bloomed exactly as she intended for the past 200 years.

Alcatraz Prison

SAN FRANCISCO, CALIFORNIA, UNITED STATES

The world's most notorious prison sits atop a lonely outcrop of rocks in the midst of a brutal and raging ocean. Its shell of steel and reinforced concrete stands shrouded in a sickly damp fog—not the most welcoming of sights to have greeted the procession of criminals doomed there to ruthless incarceration. Its dark and brooding history is filled with terror and brutality, the worst of which still lurks within its impenetrable walls.

By 1853, the Army Corps of Engineers had begun constructing a fortress in order to take advantage of the island's unique defensive position. The island proved to be decidedly inhospitable, and it wasn't long before a landslide claimed the first of many lives.

The fortress was first used as a military prison in 1861. Army deserters were incarcerated in irons in the basement cells, where living conditions were particularly grim. There was no running water or heat in the cells, and disease was rife.

In 1934, Alcatraz was designated a maximum-security prison for America's most hardened criminals. Frank Bolt had the honor of becoming prisoner number one and endured a five-year stretch for sodomy. The most famous of all Alcatraz inmates is the infamous gangster Al Capone, who entered its jaws as prisoner number eighty-five.

The regime within Alcatraz was particularly harsh. Armed guards patrolled the corridors and any inmates who failed to abide by the rules were thrown

into the tiny cells of D-block, where they were lucky to be allowed out for ten minutes a week in order to shower. Many prisoners committed suicide, preferring death to this life of deprivation and routine. The guards constantly beat prisoners, and the cells echoed with the sounds of clanging metal and terrified screams. Escape was impossible and any prisoners who attempted it were washed back to the island and smashed against the jagged rocks by an unforgiving sea.

For twenty-nine years Alcatraz reigned as America's safest prison, by which time it had truly earned the nickname "Hellcatraz." It was finally closed on March 21, 1963, and now a million people a year actually pay to visit "The Rock" and discern its grisly past.

The empty corridors and cells are filled with a terrible energy that holds within it all the fear and pain of the lives once held captive. The spirits that haunt the prison were up to their tricks long before it closed down. From 1946 to 1963, guards reported hearing sobbing and moaning coming from empty cells; there were cold spots, repulsive smells, and a "thing" with red eyes that would chase them down corridors. On many occasions the laundry room would be filled with the strong scent of smoke, choking the guards out. When they returned a few minutes later, the smell would be gone.

On one occasion a prisoner thrown into D-block was heard screaming that something with glowing red eyes was in the cell with him. His cries of terror went unheeded throughout the night. The following morning, when guards unlocked the door, they found him dead with hand marks around his neck. It was confirmed that the hand marks were not self-inflicted. Was it the evil spirit of a former inmate inflicting his rage upon the terrified soul?

In the 1940s, during a Christmas party held at the Warden's house, several guards witnessed the hair-raising apparition of a man in a gray suit sporting muttonchops. The room grew icy and still, and the fire in the stove went out. As the guards stood motionless the specter suddenly vanished.

Within the prison today the most haunted location is still D-block, or "The Hole" as it came to be known. Cell 14D is intensely cold even when the surrounding temperature is twenty degrees higher, and causes visitors to shiver violently. Upon entering cell 12D visitors report an overwhelming sensation of being watched. An evil entity lurking there has been known to place its icy fingers around the necks of many hapless victims.

The Park Rangers who now work on the island experience strange phenomena on a daily basis. They report crashing sounds, cell doors mysteriously slamming shut, unearthly screams, and the intense sensation of being watched. A psychic investigator who once visited the island reported feeling energy like none other he had ever experienced: intense feelings of fear, pain, anger, and abuse.

Visitors today can experience the overwhelming sense of dread once felt by long dead prisoners. Just book yourself a seat onboard a Red and White Fleet Ferry Service, but be sure to spare a thought for the tortured souls you leave behind once you are safely on your way home from "Hellcatraz."

Flight 401

FLORIDA, UNITED STATES

The tragedy of an airline crash is always headline news and leaves in its wake deep-rooted trauma for the survivors and heartbreak for the bereaved. But one crash left an additional legacy: it became one of the best-documented cases of a haunting in modern times. It incorporated the highly persuasive testimonies from respected professionals that covered more than twenty separate incidents.

On December 29, 1972, Flight 401, an Eastern Airlines L-1011 jumbo jet, was beginning its approach to Miami Airport with 176 passengers on board. The pilot, Captain Bob Loft, and his Second Officer, Don Repo, were carrying out routine landing procedures. A faulty warning light on the control panel began flashing, indicating a problem with the landing gear that didn't exist, and the men were temporarily distracted. The plane began descending two hundred feet per minute faster than they had calculated, and in a moment came crashing into the Florida Everglades. One hundred and one passengers died instantly. Loft and Repo were not killed outright, but Loft died in his seat before he could be pulled free from the burning wreckage. Repo died in the hospital the following day.

In the weeks following the crash, it became increasingly evident that neither of the men was ready to hang up his uniform.

Sections of Flight 401 that had not been damaged in the crash were recycled to relieve pressure on the airline manufacturer's production line. Soon a series of bizarre reports from many of the aircrafts with salvaged parts left the

industry feeling increasingly unsettled: apparently, Loft and Repo were still reporting for duty.

Testimonies from senior airline personnel, both in-flight and management, began detailing encounters with the men. A report published by the Flight Safety Foundation commented that "experienced and trustworthy pilots and crew" had reported these incidents. There was even an account by one of the vice presidents of the airline who joined a Miami-bound flight at JFK Airport in New York. He began talking to the airline captain he assumed to be taking the flight. As was common to all sightings, there was nothing ethereal about the man; he appeared very real. But the instant the vice president realized he was conversing with the late Bob Loft, the man vanished.

Several other sightings of Bob Loft were of an unresponsive, drawn, and ill-looking man in an Eastern Airlines uniform seen by several in-flight attendants and passengers. Many of these incidents had multiple witnesses, as many as twelve in at least one case. In one instance, flight attendants became so concerned about an unlisted and unresponsive passenger in airline uniform that the captain was summoned. As he approached, the captain froze, saying, "My God, it's Bob Loft!" Again, Loft instantly vanished.

The spirit of Don Repo seemed determined to ensure the safety of Eastern Airline flights even from beyond the grave. One flight engineer was carrying out his routine pre-flight inspection when he suddenly became aware that he had been joined by Repo, who told him, "You don't need to worry about the pre-flight; I've already done it." On another occasion, a flight attendant reported seeing a flight engineer repairing a galley oven. After he mentioned this to a colleague, it came out that the flight attendant on board had not carried out the repair himself, and that as far as he was aware the repair was still scheduled. Records indicated that the galley oven had been salvaged from Flight 401.

Four airline personnel on board another flight, including a flight engineer who had been a personal friend, witnessed Repo. They recognized him instantly and all reported how Repo warned them to "watch out for fire on this plane." The last leg of the flight was canceled after the plane developed serious engine faults.

In another incident, a flight was canceled before take-off after the captain and two flight attendants were left too shaken to fly. They reported having had a conversation with Bob Loft in the cockpit that ended abruptly when he suddenly vanished.

Airline authorities refused to be drawn into discussion about the ghosts of Flight 401, and recommended that any personnel who had had an unusual experience take up the airline's offer of free psychiatric treatment.

Despite its public skepticism, Eastern Airlines quietly took the costly precaution of removing all salvaged parts of Flight 401 from their fleet. The sightings have since ceased.

Hell House of New Orleans

NEW ORLEANS, LOUISIANA, UNITED STATES

T he Rue Royale is one of the most elegant streets in New Orleans. It is situated in the French Quarter and has been home to many eminent members of society. Midway along the street stands number 1140, a handsome house, exquisitely trimmed with lacy wrought-iron balconies. Its calm, stately exterior belies the extraordinary horror that once lay inside.

In 1832, Delphine LaLaurie and her husband, Dr. Louis LaLaurie, moved into the enviously situated house. Delphine had been born to prominent members of New Orleans' aristocracy and was acknowledged as a woman of remarkable beauty and intelligence. She was kindly and gracious, with a particularly melodic voice, and devoted a lot of her spare time to charitable works.

Delphine and Dr. LaLaurie began their stay on Rue Royale as a well-respected couple. They hosted magnificent dinner galas, and the cream of society vied for their invitations. Their many guests marveled at the opulent interior of their house. The large social rooms were lit with hundreds of candles hanging in ornate chandeliers. The furnishings were fashionable, made from the finest of silks, and expensive ornaments decorated every corner. The guests were waited upon by the LaLauries' large staff of slaves, with dinner served on immaculate china and musicians playing lively music. Delphine played the perfect hostess, with the impeccable manners and social graces of high breeding.

However, appearances can be deceptive, and whispered rumors of the LaLauries' mistreatment of their slaves began to circulate. Although slave

ownership was still common in those days, laws had been passed to prevent undue cruelty.

The lavish gatherings and the underlying whisperings continued until one day, in 1833, a neighbor heard terrifying screams coming from the LaLaurie house. She looked out of her window to see Delphine chasing a young slave girl in the backyard and beating her with a whip. The poor girl was stricken with fear and ran into the house with her incensed owner at her heels. She ran blindly to the top of the house, where she eventually emerged onto the roof. The fear of being caught by her mistress was obviously so great that jumping was a preferable option. She plunged to her death in front of the horrified neighbor.

Delphine was reported to the authorities and charged with abuse. She was given a miniscule fine, and the remainder of her slaves were removed from her house and sold at public auction. The unfortunate slaves were, however, bought by Delphine's relatives and returned without question to the LaLaurie house.

By now the rumors of abuse were rife, and the once coveted invitations began to be refused. It was noted that a significant number of new slaves would arrive at the LaLaurie house, but none were known to leave or to be sold. The lid was about to be lifted off a bottomless pit of evil.

In a desperate bid to bring attention to their plight, the LaLaurie cook set fire to the kitchen. She was later found to have been chained to the stove. As the fire spread, neighbors arrived to help save valuables, and the fire brigade attempted to extinguish the flames. Delphine was, by all accounts, very calm, issuing instructions for jewels, robes, furniture, and paintings to be taken out onto the street. It wasn't long before someone noticed the lack of slaves. Surely they should be there, helping to evacuate the house and scrambling to escape the flames? Delphine was dismissive, intent on saving her belongings and reluctant to allow anyone to search the house.

The fire brigade eventually brought the fire under control and began to look for the missing slaves. The search ended in the basement behind a heavily barred wooden door. The sight that met their eyes brought some of the men to their knees and set many to vomiting where they stood.

The room in the basement was filled with the remains of countless mangled and tortured slaves. Many were dead, but the most unfortunate were still alive. They were the victims of the most inhuman tortures imaginable. The

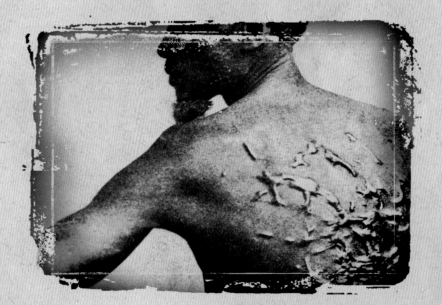

scene is almost impossible to describe. Many slaves were chained to the walls, their faces grossly disfigured. There were slaves compressed into tiny cages, unable to move a limb. Some had been sexually mutilated, and the amputated arms and legs of others were strewn about the floor and stacked onto shelves. It was a scene of utter depravity.

As the sickened firemen stumbled out onto the street and news of the carnage spread through the gathered crowd, cries for justice filled the air. In the confusion and horror of the situation, Delphine coolly climbed into her carriage and sped away. She was never heard from again.

The blackened house remained empty for years, a monument to the darkness of the human heart. Few cared to pass by on the same side of the street for fear of the hellish memories contained within reaching out to grab their souls. "*La maison est hauntée*" was the whisper that fell from lips as strange flitting shapes and unearthly noises were reported emerging from its darkened interior. It was eventually bought and restored in 1837, but the new owners fled after just a month in residence. The cries and screams of pain, maniacal laughter, and sounds of torture that filled the house after nightfall proved too much for them to bear.

The house remained empty for a further forty years until it was used for a short while as a girls' school and then later as a dance school. Various businesses passed through its tortured rooms, all of them soon abandoned. Reports of hauntings abounded, with apparitions and heart-rending screams ripping through the hollow rooms with increasing frequency. One resident was attacked in the hall by a naked black man shackled in chains, and butchered animals were seen scattered around, only to disappear of their own accord.

The house was eventually converted into upscale apartments, and during renovations numerous human skeletal remains were unearthed from under floorboards and from shallow graves around the property. The present owners have seen nothing untoward as yet. Maybe the discovery of the hidden graves appeased the persecuted souls once trapped there, or maybe they are lying low, gathering strength, lest the world forget the suffering endured within the house of hell.

The Spirits of Chickamauga Battlefield

One of the bloodiest battles of the American Civil War was fought alongside Georgia's Chickamauga Creek on September 19 and 20, 1863. It was a battle of enormous ferocity which resulted in the mass slaughter of thousands of soldiers, and left in its wake a good deal more than just blood-soaked earth.

The terrain surrounding Chickamauga Creek was rough and hostile with densely wooded areas and rocky, uneven ground. Soldiers became separated from their units and found themselves stumbling lost and alone through the forbidding woods, the muffled sounds of screams and gunfire close behind them. The fighting was shambolic and deteriorated into vicious one-on-one skirmishes, with soldiers staring into the eyes of their killers.

The terrible battle raged for two days and the bodies began to pile up. As dusk fell on day two, the last shot was fired and an eerie silence fell across the corpse-strewn land. The Confederate army, led by General Braxton Bragg, had won their last major victory of the war. The defeated Union troops withdrew, staggering behind their leader, General William Rosecrans. More than 35,000 men were killed, wounded, or reported missing, and Chickamauga Creek ran red with blood. The Union soldiers were left where they fell, in tangled heaps of rotting flesh. They were left in the open for almost two months before being hurriedly buried in shallow unmarked graves all across the battleground.

The Chickamauga National Battlefield was established in 1890 and is one of the oldest and largest battlefield parks in existence today. Although serene and peaceful during daylight hours, nightfall brings horrors to dread.

The air of Chickamauga is thick with wandering spirits trailing through the fields and darkened woods. Sounds of men moaning and crying are interspersed with shouts and screams of agony, although no one but the witness is present. There are sounds of galloping horses approaching but no horse appears. There is the most overwhelming feeling of being watched by something hiding in the shadows of the woods. The underbrush is seen to shiver inexplicably, as though something or someone is moving through it.

One well-known spirit is that of a lonely bride-to-be still dressed in her white wedding gown. Her ghostly figure is often seen drifting about the park. She is believed to be searching for the lost spirit of her slain beau so that their souls can be united in the afterlife. She is often accompanied by eerie lights and the voices and cries of women, long dead, who were seen in the days following the battle scouring the field by lantern light in the hope of finding their loved ones alive among the corpses.

Perhaps the most famous entity to haunt the battlefield is "Old Green Eyes." This rather terrifying spirit earned its nickname after scaring the daylights out of a number of hapless witnesses. Many people have encountered a pair of glowing green eyes coming towards them from out of the darkness accompanied by the moans of a man in despair. It is said that "Old Green Eyes" was a Confederate soldier whose head was blown off during the great battle. His body was never found so only his head was buried, and he now endlessly wanders the battleground searching for his missing body.

More sinister reports state that the flashing green eyes belong to an inhuman creature that was present at Chickamauga long before the Civil War. Accounts tell of the monstrous spirit being seen picking its way through the dead after the battle was over. A park ranger named Richard Tinney had a terrifying encounter with the creature while on duty one night in the 1980s. He describes feeling a strange chill descend upon him unlike anything he had ever experienced before, and then seeing green glowing eyes appear out of the gloom. He saw that the creature had long flowing hair and huge protruding fang-like teeth. The ranger was transfixed by fear until the headlights of a car appeared in the distance and the creature vanished before his eyes.

Long before the Civil War, Native Americans had lived in this region and had christened the creek *Chickamauga* meaning "River of Death." Little did they know how appropriate this name would become. To this day park maintenance workers occasionally unearth a poorly buried casualty of the war; for these poor souls, the battle is certainly not over.

The Amityville House of Horrors

AMITYVILLE, NEW YORK, UNITED STATES

There is a pretty village situated just twenty miles outside New York City. It is a beautiful waterfront community full of amazing old buildings and peaceful parks, a great place to bring up a family. It is strange, then, that its name should strike fear into the hearts of a generation of people the world over, and conjure up the horror of an evil beyond imagination. But it is not so strange when the village in question is Amityville.

Amityville will be forever tainted by the memory of events which took place in the imposing colonial-style house located at 112 Ocean Avenue. Events have been well documented and turned into books and films, and they are no less horrific for all their claims to fame.

The story begins in the fall of 1974, when police received a phone call informing them of a multiple shooting in the normally quiet village of Amityville. They arrived at 112 Ocean Avenue to find that six members of a family had been massacred in their beds. Ronald DeFeo, Sr., his wife Louise, and four of their children, Mark, John, Dawn, and Allison, had all been shot in the back with a high powered rifle. The eldest son, Ronald DeFeo, was charged with the murders and sentenced to 150 years in prison. Throughout the trial he pleaded insanity, claiming that a demonic spirit had possessed him and driven him to slay his entire family in cold blood.

After much discussion regarding the wretched and bloody history of the house, George Lutz and his wife Kathy decided that 112 Ocean Avenue could be their ideal home despite its gory past. On December 18, 1975, they moved in with their three children and the family dog Harry. From the moment they began unpacking their boxes, it became clear that all was not as it should be. Indeed their "perfect home" was shortly to become their worst imaginable nightmare.

A friend of the family, Father Ralph Pecoraro, was called in on their first day to bless their new home. He left the family outside unloading the moving trucks and went into the house to perform the blessing. Father Pecoraro left Amityville a very disturbed man. He would never fully discuss what he had experienced and only told the Lutzes that he had felt something in one of the second-floor bedrooms that he was not comfortable with and that he would rather they did not use that room as a bedroom. Meanwhile Harry the dog had been tied up at the back of the house to keep him out of the way while the family unpacked. It was discovered that he had almost hung himself in a desperate bid to leave the property. The events of the first day were nothing compared to what the family was later to endure.

As each new day in the house unfolded, it became clear that something was very wrong inside the Lutzes' new home. Strange nauseating smells permeated the house, the toilet bowls turned black, and a sticky dark substance dripped from keyholes in the doors. A green, jelly-like goo dribbled from the walls, and swarms of houseflies gathered time and again in the second-floor room where the priest had felt most threatened.

The noises came next, with loud footsteps marching throughout the house and the sound of the front door being slammed shut in the middle of the night. Whenever George ran down to investigate he would always find the door locked with the dog still asleep in front of it. George began to hear another strange nighttime noise, like the distant sound of an out-of-tune brass band. The sound plagued him night after night, and on investigation he would find rugs rolled up and furniture moved. George's personality began to change; he would wake at precisely 3:15 A.M. each morning and have to go outside to check the boathouse. He became sick and listless and virtually gave up bathing. Kathy and the kids began fighting and arguing with one another, and Kathy was woken night after night by the most horrifying nightmares.

Apparitions started to manifest inside the house, and Kathy would often feel something grasping her from behind. Shadows began to drift out of corners. The family would see things staring in at them through the windows at night and hoofprints would be found outside the window in the morning. Once, when Kathy threw a chair at the staring eyes the high-pitched squeal of a pig shattered the silent night air. A friend suggested they go throughout the house reciting the Lord's Prayer, but when they attempted this, a multitude of disembodied voices screamed at them to stop.

The final straw for the family came when their young daughter, Missy, developed an attachment to a mysterious imaginary friend named Jodie. Apparently, Jodie could change shape and was fond of telling the four-year-old Missy that she was going to live in the house forever.

Finally, twenty-eight days after moving into their new home, the family had had enough and decided to leave while they still had their wits about them. The house seemed to sense this, and as the Lutzes ran around grabbing clothes and personal belongings the walls began to undulate and groan, and the temperature inside rose to boiling and then fell to freezing. As George ran for the door he saw a hooded figure standing silently at the top of the stairs with its finger pointed directly at him.

The controversy surrounding the haunting has raged for years with many people believing the whole thing to have been a hoax. However, the Lutzes never profited from their experience. Investigators found that the house had been built upon an area once inhabited by Shinnecock Indians who had used the place to isolate the sick and insane members of their tribe.

Who knows the truth? But the last word should go to George Lutz who is recorded as having said, "It's my prayer that other people never have to go through such a thing. But if you know someone that does, the hardest thing for those people is the loss of being able to communicate with anyone else about it. Not being able to find anyone that can intelligently help them. It's not talked about, it's not understood . . . and when it happens to you, you become an alien to everyone else."

Phantom of the Forests

T he Windigo is a dark and terrifying entity rooted in the earliest legends of the Native Indians of Canada. This fearful spirit looms large in the lives of the Algonquin people, which include the Ojibwa, Cree, and Blackfoot tribes. These tribes now live on reservations in the Northwest Territories, Ontario, Manitoba, Saskatchewan, Alberta, and the outer regions of Quebec. The formless and vengeful spirit of the Windigo is the stuff of nightmares. It lurks within the deepest, darkest forests, silently hovering and watching. It is a phantom of hunger, hunting out lonely wanderers to attack and possess. No other evil spirit has ever evoked such terror in a people.

The Windigo is a ghost of winter, howling in the bitter wind and turning the hearts of victims into blocks of ice. The legend states that during harsh winters, when food was scarce, the spirit of a Windigo would enter a person, causing them to become violent and antisocial, with a taste for human flesh. The only way to get rid of the malevolent spirit would be to set fire to the body of its host.

The Windigo can fly through the forests and melt into the winds, moving faster than the human eye can follow. It is possessed of a supernatural strength and can kill a person with a single glare.

You would be forgiven for assuming that the Windigo is a phantom grown from the seeds of imagination, a folkloric tale passed on from generation to generation, or a story told by Indian medicine men in their winter camps to fill the minds of empty-bellied children. It is a story rooted in fact, with numerous historical accounts documenting the trials of Windigo-possessed people.

The earliest of these accounts dates back to the 1700s when an explorer named David Thompson witnessed such a trial while traveling through the Lake of the Woods region. A young Indian hunter had been taken over by the spirit of a Windigo and was battling with a desire to eat his own sister. A decision was taken by the tribal council, and the young hunter was first strangled by his father then thrown onto a huge fire where his body was burnt to ashes. Not a single bone was left remaining, ensuring that the evil spirit could not return to the world of mankind.

Many reports of the Windigo came from hard-headed frontiersmen who were not given to superstition. Their lives were far too difficult and rooted in practical concerns to spare a thought for supernatural imaginings.

One of the best-documented cases of a Windigo haunting took place in the Five Lakes Region in North Eastern Alberta. In 1746, a group of settlers staked claim to various plots of land close to an already established but secretive camp. The people of this camp indulged in weird ritualistic ceremonies, and wild rumors circulated about them. Not long after establishing their homes, the body of one of the new farmers was found butchered and partially eaten, the apparent victim of a grizzly bear attack. Three men were dispatched to hunt down the bear and headed into the forest near the mysterious camp. They never returned and the suspicion grew that the strange goings on within the nearby camp were to blame for the death of the farmer and the missing hunters.

The settlers' anger grew and they eventually approached William Blake, the leader of the camp, to demand that he and his followers leave the area. Their demand was refused, so they surrounded the camp and sealed it off, ensuring that livestock and crops could not be tended. After a particularly long and bitter winter the settlers broke into the camp and found the entire community, including William Blake, dead. The bodies, with limbs ripped off and partially eaten, were strewn about the place. An orgy of cannibalism had obviously taken place, and women and children had been devoured in a frenzied banquet. The settlers torched the camp in an attempt to erase the horror from their minds, and William Blake and his community were never spoken of again.

The years passed and a century later the town of Fort Kent was built on the fertile land where the old settlers had once lived. An English doctor named Thomas Burton moved to the town with his wife, Katie, and soon established a successful medical practice. At first the town and its people seemed to flourish, but in the winter of 1920 the dreams and happiness of the townspeople were irrevocably shattered.

A great plague of rats invaded the town and many people were struck down with deadly and mysterious illnesses. The winter was the longest and coldest ever recorded, with families trapped dying and alone in their homes while their livestock perished in the killer snows. Thomas Burton did all he could for his patients but when his own wife fatally succumbed to disease he gave up all hope and barricaded himself into his house.

After a few months he reappeared in the community a completely changed man. He was wild and unkempt, a shadow of his former self. He would stalk the streets at night, hiding in the shadows, and, most chillingly of all, he insisted he was now called William Blake, a name which had not been uttered in the area for over a hundred years, and of which he certainly would never have heard.

On a flat and lifeless fall evening in October 1921, the possessed body of Thomas Burton systematically broke into every house in the town and slaughtered and ate parts of all but eleven residents. Had the once hardworking doctor been invaded by the spirit of a one-hundred-year-old Windigo? The Royal Canadian Mounted Police attempted to suppress the news, such was the terror it evoked. Thomas Burton was executed for his crimes, but his body was never burned. Does this mean that the vile and savage demon of the forest has been left to wander, searching for its next victim? The Native Indians of Canada certainly believe so, and the cursed spirit of the Windigo continues to do battle with the suffering souls of men.

The Haunted Hotel

BANFF, CANADA

The Banff Springs Hotel lies in the heart of the Rocky Mountains in western Canada. It is one of the most luxurious hotels in the world and is prized not only for its services and amenities, but for its breathtaking location. It is surrounded by majestic mountains, scenic rivers and lakes, and wonderfully therapeutic hot springs.

The hotel was constructed in 1888 by the Canadian Pacific Railroad as it carved its way through the wilderness of the mountains. The potential of the location was noted by William Van Horne, Vice President of the CPR, and he ordered the building of the sumptuous 250-room hotel.

Despite its obvious attractiveness, the hotel hides some dark and ghoul-ish secrets within its vast and lavish interior. During the construction of the building, workmen mistakenly created a room with neither doors nor windows. Working within a tight schedule and an even tighter budget, they decided the safest course of action would be to hide their blunder and confess to no one. So the Banff Springs was completed with only the workmen aware of the existence of an extra room.

The hotel proved incredibly popular, attracting visitors from all over the world, but it wasn't long before guests reported seeing strange and shadowy apparitions drifting down the corridor bordering the hidden room. A mist would appear in the surrounding rooms and a phantom bellhop would mate-rialize and ask the terrified guests in a disturbingly hoarse whisper whether he could fetch them anything. A fire broke out in the hotel in 1926, and it was

54

only then that the hidden room was discovered. It was, of course, completely empty and had been inaccessible, but the hotel management was convinced that its existence was somehow responsible for the unnerving phenomena that had been occurring in the adjacent corridor. They surmised that, as the room had been empty, the lost spirits of workmen who had died during the hotel's construction had decided to take up residence.

The hotel was rebuilt in 1928 and became known as the Castle of the Rockies. The removal of the hidden room did, indeed, dispel the shadows of the work-men, but the ghoulish bellhop continues in his duties. He is a conscientious worker and has even been known to open doors for guests who have forgotten their keys. He is now affectionately known as "Sam."

There is a place within the hotel which holds an even darker mystery. Room 873 does not appear on the hotel registry and employees are forbidden to talk of it. Its doorway has been walled up, although you can still see the space where it used to be. It is rumored that a family was murdered in this room and the hideous cries of their pain and terror petrified all subsequent residents. Hotel cleaners refused to enter the room after trying on numerous occasions to remove child-sized fingerprints from the mirrors. No matter how hard they polished, the tiny prints would appear again and again. Room 873 was sealed and the hotel once again harbored a hidden room.

Sam the bellhop is not the only spirit to wander the plushly carpeted and expensively scented rooms of the Banff Springs Hotel. He has been joined by the vision of a woman in a white wedding dress with a hideously disfigured face. She is seen by visitors descending the central staircase and is thought to be the ghost of a bride whose wedding took place at the hotel. She had the staircase filled with hundreds of lighted candles so her entrance into the reception would be wonderfully romantic. However, the heavy lace of her dress caught on a candle and she entered the reception as a fireball.

For all its murky mysteries, the Castle of the Rockies is a truly awesome building in a spectacular location where you can be sure of the warmest of welcomes, especially from the ever-attentive "Sam."

La Llorona

For centuries the children of Mexico have been terrified by the story of *La Llorona*. Part pitiful banshee, part angry spirit, she has become legendary, and her tale is a central piece of Mexican folklore. But to dismiss *La Llorona* as nothing more than legend would be to ignore the experiences of many hundreds of Mexicans through the centuries, who have had terrifying encounters with the grief-stricken spirit.

Over time, the woman at the heart of this haunting has become lost in myriad variations of her life story. Most versions share some common threads, however. It is widely believed that at some point in the sixteenth century, before the fall of the Aztecs, a beautiful young widow, often attributed as living in Juarez, was struggling to raise her three young children despite her poverty. She met and fell in love with a wealthy young man. She placed all her hopes for providing a better life for herself and her children on him, but she was to be bitterly disappointed. The man had no desire to tie himself down with a widow and another man's offspring, and he left her. Driven to distraction by her desperate poverty, the woman lost control of her senses, and drowned her children in the Rio Bravo.

Almost instantly, she realized the full horror of her actions. Screaming and tearing at her hair, the woman ran all night along the river banks, desperately searching for her children. She never found them. What happened next varies from story to story. Either she drowned herself in the river, or she was set upon by an angry mob who threw her into the river. Either way, she shared the same fate as her children.

The first recorded sightings of her ghost date back as early as 1550. Locals in Juarez described hearing her devastating cries piercing the night and saw her wraith gliding up and down the river banks, locked in an eternal search for her lost children. Before long, she was dubbed *La Llorona* (which means "the bereaved" or "the one who cries") and her spirit was blamed for an increasing number of drowning incidents in the Rio Bravo. To this day, the name of *La Llorona* is whispered whenever any drowned corpse fished out of the river.

More than five hundred years later sightings of the apparition are widespread. Reports come from all over Mexico and beyond, to New Mexico and Texas. All sightings are on or near waterways or drainage ditches. She is seen either all in white or in black, and is often described as wailing, "*¡O hijos mios!*" or "*¡Ay mis hijos!*" (Oh my children!). In all reports she makes the same chilling, unearthly cry. The twisting of the spirit into that of a banshee has happened over the course of centuries, with little of any note to substantiate claims that those who see her are themselves marked for death.

La Llorona has also been associated with attempting to drown children or drunken young men, although it is widely accepted that this has been a convenient tool with which to warn both of these sections of the population away from the water's edge. Modern sightings do, however, reveal *La Llorona's* preoccupation with children and families. Several witnesses report the sound of hair-raising cries coming from their infant's nursery, only to discover their baby sound asleep and the noise to have shifted to an undeterminable location outside their home.

Sightings along the waterways are most commonly reported during late October and early November, usually during a full moon. The unearthly cries always precede sightings. In many places, teenagers dare themselves to walk the river banks at night, in search of the spirit. A group of teenagers in El Paso, Texas, on the Mexican border, reported being terrified one night in the 1980s during a nighttime expedition along the dark, deserted banks of the river (the Rio Bravo is called the Rio Grande in the U.S.). As they approached the underside of a bridge across the water, the quiet of the night was suddenly broken by a blood-curdling sobbing and the same frantic babbling reported in so many other sightings. The terrified youngsters fled back to the safety of their car, unwilling to meet *La Llorona* face to face.

There is a final interpretation to the story of the wailing spirit that bemoans her lost children all over Mexico. Some argue that several sightings of this spirit were recorded before the tale of the wronged woman who drowned her children. The ghost, they say, appeared first as a premonition of the impending fall of the Aztecs, prior to the Spanish colonization. Her tragic cries for her lost children were for all her people, not her own direct offspring, and warned them of the events that then took place in 1527 when the Aztec Empire fell to the Spanish. After colonization, her cries continued to echo her sadness at the loss of Aztec independence, but were misinterpreted to become the legend of *La Llorona*.

The truth behind the identity of the grief-stricken phantom remains to be seen; but after five hundred years, its lonely lament continues all over Mexico. Any unlucky enough to hear it agree that it is a cry unlike any they have ever heard, and one they are not likely to forget.

The Haunted Bank

Mexico City's most eerie haunting is located in the most unpredictable of settings. In the heart of the city is the fashionable sector known as the Zona Rosa, so called because many of the buildings were once painted pink. Trendy bars and stylish restaurants bustle with city folk from the financial sector that has had its base there since the earliest days of the city.

One of the most impressive buildings in the area is the Centro Bancomer building. It bristles with life, as more than ten thousand people work within its walls each day.

At night it is little more than a concrete shell. Floor upon floor of desks stand empty. Only the occasional loyal employee, staying late, or small teams of cleaning or security staff rattle around inside its cavernous interior. But it is at night that another unearthly resident has begun to make its presence known, terrorizing those who are unfortunate enough to encounter it.

The canteen reserved for the senior management of the bank is plush and well equipped, and the catering staff who work there are highly valued. So when two of the cooks resigned, saying that a recurring encounter in the kitchen had left them both too traumatized to continue to work, the management took their claims very seriously.

The women began, reluctantly at first, to tell a story that was to leave the management dumbfounded. They explained that while remaining behind after the day's cooking had finished, they had been troubled on several occa-

sions by a sudden and distinct drop in the air temperature. Gradually, they would become aware of the sound of footsteps. There was something that was both familiar and yet strangely out of context in the rapid, light tread of what they said sounded like little feet upon the tiled floor. The steps were too light to be an adult's; the women felt certain they were listening to the sound of a running child. On the final occasion, as the women's sense of uneasiness heightened, a small boy appeared from out of nowhere, running and skipping. He passed directly in front of them and then vanished, appearing to "melt" into the wall at the far end of the kitchen. Nothing their employers said could persuade the women to return to work.

On one of the lower floors, office workers staying late alone in the building began to report bizarre electrical phenomena. Lights switched on and off at random and several employees were startled by the sight of various items on their desk, including stationery or drink bottles, appearing to move across the table in front of their eyes.

One night, a member of the bank's managerial team met *El Chamaco* (the little kid) face-to-face. The employee was working late and alone in his office in the basement of the building. His concentration was suddenly interrupted by the noise of a considerable disturbance outside his office. He ignored it for as long as he could, but eventually his curiosity overwhelmed him and he went to investigate. The instant he opened his door, the noise stopped. Taking a look around, he saw no one and found nothing amiss. He returned to his desk.

Again, the silence was broken by rapid, running footsteps and the sound of something being thrown or slammed down. He lost his temper, shouting at whoever was creating such a distraction. Suddenly, a large cork notice-board fell to the floor, startling him. As he reached up to replace it, he saw a wraith-like but distinct image of a little boy's mischievous face grinning down at him from the ceiling.

It was the experiences of several night security staff at the bank which add a final eerie chapter to this story. In the early hours of the morning, around 1 A.M., the security guards began to receive a series of phone calls from a little boy. The guards were disconcerted by such an apparently young child being up alone at such an hour. But it was the repetition of the calls that made the guards connect the voice to the other strange occurrences at the bank. The request made by the child prompted the guards to offer the company a possible motive for the mischievous spirit's unearthly antics. The child's voice said simply, "Play with me!"

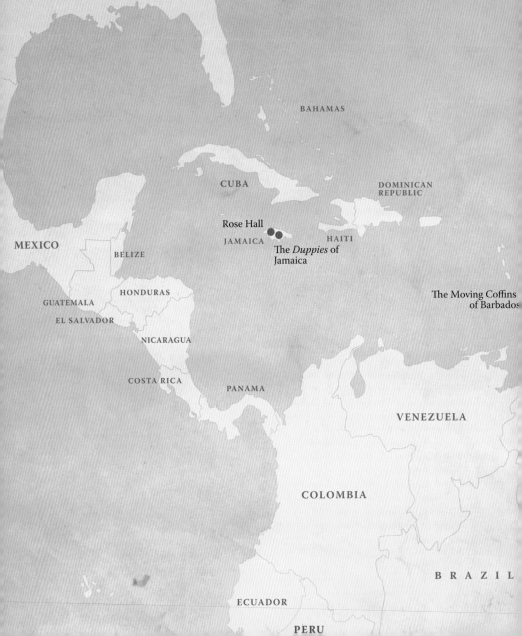

UNITED STATES OF
AMERICA

BAHAMAS

CUBA

DOMINICAN
REPUBLIC

Rose Hall

JAMAICA   HAITI

The *Duppies* of
Jamaica

MEXICO

BELIZE   The Moving Coffins
of Barbados

HONDURAS

GUATEMALA

EL SALVADOR

NICARAGUA

VENEZUELA

COSTA RICA

PANAMA

COLOMBIA

BRAZIL

ECUADOR

PERU

Caribbean

On the islands of the Caribbean, centuries of human-rights neglect created a difficult, violent past. Little surprise that paranormal incidents there are often disturbing: the islands' spirits have a great deal to be angry about.

Rose Hall

MONTEGO BAY, JAMAICA

A nnie Palmer was a beautiful woman who traveled halfway across the world to marry a wealthy plantation owner, but ended her days as an adulteress, a voodoo witch, and a murderess. Her reputation was so formidable, and her presence in the plantation house so strong, that locals still protect themselves against her evil spirit.

In the Jamaican economy of the nineteenth century, two basic commodities—sugar and slaves—were king. The potential for amassing wealth in this way was substantial. Rose Hall, the most impressive of all the "great houses" on the island dating from this period, stands testament to this. It was built in the latter part of the eighteenth century for the colossal sum of $55,000. The 6,600 acres of the plantation at Rose Hall were worked by 2,000 slaves.

For a woman in this period, there was only one path to this wealth: marriage. A young Parisian woman, Annie Mae Patterson, inherited the position of mistress of the plantation when, in 1820, she married John Palmer, the plantation owner. Annie was petite, feisty, and exquisitely beautiful. Being a wealthy woman in a world of enforced labor and piracy put her in a dangerous position; Annie quickly learned that she needed to get tough if she was to get on.

Annie quickly gained a reputation as a fearsome mistress. She had also acquired a secret passion. Raised by a nursemaid from Haiti, she had been tutored in more than manners: she had become an expert in the dark art of voodoo. The dungeon below the house was the setting for her witchcraft. Annie would grind the bones of dead babies to a fine powder for use in her spells.

She had a voracious sexual appetite and little desire to commit to a lifelong marriage. Quickly tiring of her husband, she poisoned him in his bed and began to take many lovers. Annie Palmer married twice again, and both men met gruesome ends. She stabbed her second husband and poured boiling oil in his ears. The third husband, she strangled. It seems by this time, she had developed a liking for a more "'hands-on" method of attack. In each case, she crept into her husband's bedroom at night and murdered him while he was sleeping. At four-feet eleven-inches tall, she would have needed this advantage; she could never have overpowered them while they were awake. After the death of each husband (all, ostensibly, victims of yellow fever and all buried beneath palm trees on the edge of the plantation, bordering the beach), Annie inherited yet more wealth. Evidently, she aimed to marry again, often boasting, "If I survive, I'll marry five." How prophetic her boast turned out to be.

Unknown to Annie, the overseer of the slaves at the plantation was also a voodoo practitioner. When he realized Annie's lustful attentions were focused on his daughter's fiancé, he made preparations to protect him from her. Overcome with anger, the overseer burst into Annie's bedroom.

What voodoo was summoned by both parties that night can never be known, but the battle killed them both. Annie was buried on the estate in an unmarked grave. Keeping with voodoo tradition, a cross was placed at three of the four sides to contain her powers to her grave. The fourth side was left unprotected so that her spirit could wander.

After Annie Palmer's death, the house changed hands three times, but then fell into a hundred-year-long period of abandonment. The story of the White Witch of Rose Hall lived on, putting the fear of God into the islanders, so that in all that time, the house was never vandalized nor pillaged, despite standing empty and in ruins. Islanders tell of local children fleeing from the house in terror because of strange bloodstains and *duppies* (ghosts).

In the 1960s the house was bought by wealthy Americans, who began renovations instantly. The disturbances and poltergeist activity was so substantial, however, that a workforce had to be brought in from off the island, because no locals would work there. The disappearance of tools, and their subsequent reappearance in inaccessible places, was an almost daily occurrence. Men would constantly answer to their names, only to discover that no one else was there. The sound of ancient music playing was also reported. But most ominously, the wooden floors in three of the upstairs bedrooms had to be repeatedly sanded, as each time the workers left a perfectly sanded floor at the end of the working day, they would return the following morning to find the reappearance of an old blood stain.

Visitors to the house today continue to report many strange phenomena. Most common is the sound of rapid footsteps down empty staircases and corridors. Electrical abnormalities are also commonplace: rooms will be floodlit or plunged into darkness at random intervals. A display at the site shows the photographs from many visitors who have developed images of spectral heads in Annie's bed, or sinister dark forms materializing at the bedside. The dungeons give off the most malevolent resonances of all. Many report sensations of fear and the smell of old blood. Some hear the faint cries of babies, and whispered, barely audible voices. Most feel the chill in the atmosphere there; few remain long.

Very few original artifacts could be saved from Annie's era. Though nothing had been looted, time and the damp salty air had caused too much damage. One of the few exceptions was an original mirror that hangs in a downstairs room. It is chilling to see just how many of the strange photographs sent in by visitors center around wraith-like faces reflected in this mirror. Others describe seeing the figure of a male slave, fleetingly passing behind them in their reflection.

Today the guides who take tour parties around Rose Hall punctuate their talks with a series of strange claps and gestures designed to ward off the spirit of Annie Palmer. Her formidable presence continues to exert the threat of unspeakable terror.

The Duppies of Jamaica

In many cultures the existence of the spirit world is accepted as fact, and people's everyday lives are peppered with rituals and beliefs which take into account the needs of their ghostly companions. Jamaica is a particularly religious country with at least ten churches per square mile. It is also a country rich in superstitions and where *obeah* (the Jamaican version of voodoo) is still relatively common.

In Jamaican lore a *duppy* is the shadow of a dead person, and it is a hugely feared spirit. *Duppies* are said to be pure evil and can be conjured up if coins and rum are thrown onto graves. A *duppy*'s breath can make you sick, and its touch can cause a seizure.

Jamaicans from both ends of the social spectrum are highly suspicious of these evil spirits, and are willing to perform primitive rituals in order to protect themselves. The blood of white chickens is often daubed inside homes to ward off *duppies*, and many people refuse to enter a home if this precaution has not been taken.

Duppies regularly harm people, and *duppy*-induced injuries are often cited as an excuse to miss work. *Duppy boxing* (being slapped in the face by a *duppy*) is commonplace, and many people have been known to develop palsies and disfigurements after being attacked in this way. Reports of persons being stoned by *duppies* are widespread, and can be found throughout Jamaican history.

In 1895, a Jesuit missionary named Reverend Abraham Emerick arrived in Jamaica and spent ten years working in the missions in the heart of the mountains. He had first-hand experience of the stone-throwing *duppies*.

Reverend Emerick often journeyed to remote missions in order to administer his teachings. On one occasion, while traveling to Alva mission in the Dry Harbor Mountains, he was met by a hysterical group of local people warning him against continuing on his journey. A *duppy* had been haunting the mission school for over a week and terrible noises had been heard in and around the building. Local people had been stationed around the school to keep watch and had witnessed stones being thrown, seemingly from out of nowhere. The teacher at the school had been driven from his rooms, and he testified that a malevolent *duppy* was, indeed, responsible. He was convinced the stones were not thrown by human beings, since after smashing one window a stone would turn in a completely different direction in order to smash another.

The Reverend continued to the mission to see for himself if the stories were true. Upon arriving he found the building and the school empty, vandalized, and littered with stones. The place was quiet and strangely still, so he entered the school building to investigate the damage. As he stood surveying the wreckage a few small pebbles began to fall around him, like hailstones bouncing on the ground. The trickle grew to a heavy shower and the pebbles turned to stones. He was soon being bombarded by spectral missiles, so he turned and ran from the building in fright. The stone throwing followed him out of the mission and some distance down the road, where he took refuge in a nearby house. There was a family of six living in the house and they were overcome by terror as the stones were fired into their home, breaking windows and various ornaments. The stones seemed to come from all directions, and just as the Reverend and the family could bear no more, the throwing stopped. It seemed as though this particular *duppy* had had its fair share of fun.

The Reverend Emerick also recounted a time when he was called to a young Jamaican woman who was dying from a serious illness. As he began to administer to her, an arm reached around from behind him and slapped the poor woman with such force that her head fell sideways from the pillow. The Reverend turned quickly, but found the room empty save for himself and his patient. He dismissed the incident as a figment of his overwrought imagination, and once again prepared to administer to the dying woman. The arm once more reached around from behind him and this time threw the woman to the floor. In a panic, the Reverend searched wildly around the room for the perpetrator, but found he was still alone. On turning to help the woman back into bed, he found her dead, her vacant eyes still staring towards an unseen horror.

The Jamaicans certainly have cause to fear the native *duppy*, and it would be hard to dismiss all of the extraordinary manifestations. It is as well that they have developed strategies for dealing with this spirit and are aware of their own human limitations.

The Moving Coffins
of Barbados

Nestled on the top of a breezy hill overlooking the startling blue of the Caribbean is the quiet graveyard of Christ Church Parish in southern Barbados. It is the unlikely setting for one of the world's greatest unsolved mysteries. It is an imposing graveyard, all the more so for its envious location and expensively constructed tombs. One of these grand vaults lies at the heart of this sinister mystery.

During the 1800s, at the height of the slave trade, fortunes were being made in the rum and sugar markets. Rich plantation owners showed off their wealth and power by erecting majestic homes and government buildings on a grand scale. Their highly conspicuous displays of affluence even extended to the afterlife.

The vault of our story was carved in stone and built using coral and concrete. Large stone blocks were cemented together, creating walls that were nearly two feet thick. The entrance was sealed off by an enormous slab of blue marble. It was a most prestigious resting place, built by the Honorable James Elliot, and its first occupant was his wife, Elizabeth, who died on May 14, 1792. A few years later the vault was purchased by the Walrond family and was opened to bury the body of Mrs. Thomasina Goddard. Oddly, the coffin of its first occupant was found to be missing and the reason for its disappearance never solved.

The vault was subsequently handed over to the Chase family. The elder of the family was Colonel Thomas Chase, a brutish giant of a man known for his sadistic behavior towards slaves and his own family.

THE CHASE VAULT

The first Chase family member to be buried was baby Mary Anna Marie Chase. She died, aged two, on February 22, 1808, the cause of death unrecorded. Her pitifully small lead coffin was placed in the vault and the marble slab concreted into place. Four years later in 1812, her older sister Dorcas died under very strange circumstances. It was widely believed she starved herself to death, unable to live with the bullying and abuse at the hands of her father, Colonel Chase. This belief was never substantiated. Her lead coffin was added to the vault.

A mere month later, the tyrannical colonel himself died, and the pallbearers once again chipped away the concrete seal to open the vault. An astonishing sight met their eyes—both the girls' coffins had been seemingly thrown about the vault and were now lying in a haphazard fashion across the floor, one coffin left upside down. It was thought at first that grave robbers had carried out this unholy act, but there being no valuables were buried in the vault, and the fact that the marble entrance slab was still concreted into place left people shaking their heads in puzzlement. Nevertheless, the sisters' coffins were straightened, the colonel's coffin was added, and the vault was sealed once more.

On September 25, 1816, the vault was again unsealed to bury the body of eleven-year-old Charles Brewster Ames. The coffins inside had again been violently disturbed. Even the 240-pound lead coffin of Colonel Chase had been flung around. A horrified unease settled in people's hearts, and the story spread throughout the district. Fifty-two days later, when Samuel Brewster was due to be buried in the vault, a number of witnesses examined the outside of the tomb prior to opening. They could see nothing amiss. The tomb was airtight and waterproof, and it could not be accessed by man or beast without breaking the concrete seal on the entrance. But yet again, once the vault was opened, the mourners were mortified to discover it in chaos. The only coffin not to have been moved was the wooden coffin of Thomasina Goddard. It had, however, sustained great damage after being knocked about by the other coffins. Poor Mrs. Goddard's skeleton was found protruding from her coffin.

The mystery of the moving coffins had, by this time, reached the ears of the Governor, Lord Combermere. He decided to calm the situation and solve the puzzle once and for all.

After ascertaining that the vault was impenetrable from the outside, he ordered the inside floor to be sprinkled with sand to allow human or animal footprints to show up as evidence of intrusion. He then ordered the vault to be sealed and, as an added precaution, pressed his own governor's seal into the fresh cement (the idea being that if a perpetrator were to open the vault, then try to seal it again, he would be unable to reproduce the governor's seal).

By now the vault had a deeply disturbing reputation, with reports of strange sounds and howls heard coming from inside it at night. The governor, having left it in peace for a couple of years, decided to complete his investigation. Gathering together a group of able-bodied men, including eight slaves and two masons, and a crowd of about a hundred, he proceeded to the churchyard to open the vault. He at first ordered a methodical inspection of the outside of the vault and noted the mortar around the entrance was intact, the governor's seal still in place. After chipping away the cement, the heavy marble slab was rolled to one side with great effort. The crowd held its breath as Lord Combermere peered inside. To his utter horror the coffins were totally awry. One coffin had been leaning against the door causing the difficulty in opening. Mary Anna's lead coffin had been flung so violently onto the wall that a piece had chipped off. There were, however, no footprints or pawprints on the sand. The Chase family could take no more and had the coffins in the vault removed and buried separately in the graveyard.

The vault has since lain peacefully empty in the sun. We can only hope that the souls of the Chase family are enjoying a similar repose.

UNITED
STATES OF
AMERICA

BAHAMAS

CUBA

MEXICO

DOMINICAN
REPUBLIC

HAITI

JAMAICA

BELIZE
HONDURAS

GUATEMALA

NICARAGUA

EL SALVADOR

PANAMA

COSTA RICA

VENEZUELA

GUYANA
SURINAME
FRECH
GUIANA

COLOMBIA

The Carib Temple

ECUADOR

B R A Z I L

PERU

The House of
Count Lemo

BOLIVIA

The Haunting of
Maria José Ferreira

PARAGUAY

C H I L E

House of Laughter

URUGUAY

A R G E N T I N A

South America

From the ice-capped majesty of the Andes to the vast tropical rainforests, South America is a continent rich in vibrant cultures, ancient histories, and breathtaking beauty. Hidden amongst all this are tales whose chilling paranormal resonance is so often the consequence of man's brutality against man.

The House of Count Lemo

PUNO, PERU

The city of Puno lies comfortably on the banks of Lake Titicaca in the ancient country of Peru. It is a beautiful place, full of bright, clean streets and friendly people. There is a wonderfully fresh sharpness in the air owing to the city's high altitude and close proximity to the mountains. In a place so dazzling and clear it is hard to imagine the existence of a dark and evil presence. But in the center of town, on the corner of the Plaza de Armas, across from the cathedral, there stands the crumbling ruins of an old Spanish adobe building. This was once the home of the *Conde de Lemos* (Viceroy of Peru), and it is the most feared place in the whole neighborhood.

During the seventeenth century, the *Conde de Lemos* was known to be a particularly ruthless despot. In 1657, two brothers, Jose and Gasper Salcedo, discovered the Layakakota gold mines and soon became two of the richest men in Latin America. The iron-handed Count Lemos could not bear to be outshone and sent in his armies to capture the Layakakota mines.

Hearing word of the armies' approach, the Salcedo brothers and their families barricaded themselves into the mine with supplies of food and ammunition. The army surrounded the mine and a siege began. After several weeks the food ran out and the people holed up in the mine began to starve. To save them from further suffering the women and children were sent out into the waiting arms of the Count. Showing no mercy, the depraved Count murdered them all in front of the entrance to the mine and in full view of those still inside. When the Salcedos's ammunition finally ran out the Count had them burned alive inside the mine before declaring his victory.

His evil lives on and the house on the Plaza is still home to his restless spirit. Strange unexplained lights can be seen flitting from room to room, loud bangs and roars of anger can be heard from out on the street. There is a police station next door to the house and a small shop on the other side. Police will walk around the block to get to the shop rather than pass in front of the house of terror.

Many people have attempted to live there, but all have left after experiencing enormous amounts of ill fortune. One resident claimed to have been visited nightly by the Count. She would wake in the darkness to find his presence hovering above her, his evil eyes peering down. As soon as she screamed or turned on a light, he would disappear.

Many past residents regularly felt a heavy hand clamping down on their shoulder. They would turn to confront the assailant, and the room would, of course, be empty. Families with young children have been unable to stay in the house for more than a night without the children becoming wildly disturbed and speechless with terror. Children seem to be particularly sensitive to the presence of the Count's evil spirit, sensing his cold heart and threatening lack of morality. Occupant after occupant found themselves battling against illness and financial misfortune. It would seem even after death the Count could not bear to see others profit while he himself languished.

A young couple spent the first night of their honeymoon in the company of the Count. They were the last people to experience his malevolence at close quarters. They were accomplished sailors and after a particularly noisy and frightening night they took a boat out onto Lake Titicaca. There were high winds that day, the boat capsized, and the two excellent swimmers both drowned.

The house of Count Lemos has remained empty ever since, a dark stain bleeding into the center of Puno.

The House of Laughter

It is not only the tragedies and violence of centuries past which leave their mark on our modern world; victims of the most recent heinous events also attempt to communicate their suffering to us.

In 1973, the military authorities of Chile, under the leadership of General Pinochet, staged a violent coup and seized power over the country. The new military government implemented extensive regression and carried out summary executions of political prisoners.

In 1977, the National Information Center was created to gather information pertaining to any possible political dissension. It established detention centers where prisoners were taken for interrogation and its methods were so secret that the locations of these centers were not known. Thousands of prisoners were tortured on account of their alleged political activities. The victims came from a broad spectrum of Chilean society and included teachers, lawyers, students, peasants, doctors, and shantytown dwellers. The tortures meted out were particularly vicious. The detainees were subjected to beatings, electric shocks, rape, sleep deprivation, and burns on their genitals. A large proportion of victims "disappeared."

In the 1980s, one of the detention centers was identified. It was an ancient mansion house located on Pedro de Valdivia, close to the University of Vina del Mar. It had been given the nickname *Casa de la Risa* (House of Laughter) on account of the music which blared out from its interior both day and night. Prisoners were taken here and locked into small dark cells measuring no more

than five square feet before their regime of torture began. The loud music drowned out their screams and many never left.

Construction workers recently arrived to dismantle the condemned building, and as demolition operations commenced, they began to see and hear strange things. The workers slept in separate rooms on their first night in the house, but heard such disturbing sounds that they shared a room on subsequent nights. They were awakened by the sound of pounding on the windows, strange voices, snatches of loud music, and the occasional sound of a child crying. One workman admitted to having been grabbed from behind by an invisible force.

As work progressed the hidden secrets of the house were gradually revealed. A series of tunnels and strange passageways came to light; there were false doors which led nowhere and the workmen were witness to the unearthing of the torture dungeon. The anguished voices continued to shout and many workers left the job unable to shake off the cloak of horror that had wrapped itself around them.

The "House of Laughter" was eventually razed to the ground, its secrets buried under a pile of rubble. The fact that extensive torturing was carried out under Pinochet's rule has now been acknowledged, but the souls of the "disappeared" have yet to exact their revenge.

The Haunting of Maria José Ferreira

This is a story that is set against the complex spiritual backdrop of the largest nation on the South American continent. It is the story of a young girl from an ordinary Christian family, tormented to death by a spirit driven by revenge.

Brazil is the largest Roman Catholic country in the world: more than one hundred million of its citizens declare themselves Catholics. Brazilians are usually baptized and married in the Roman Catholic Church, but beyond that many have adopted a popularized form of the religion, whose spirituality that combines the essential tenets of the Church with a combination of different beliefs inherited from religious cults. This has resulted in a socially acceptable form of witchcraft in Brazil, known as *Umbanda*, which blends the practices of the spiritualist church with the beliefs of Roman Catholicism. *Umbanda* focuses on spirit possession. The congregation gathers in open arenas around a central sacred area. An altar is adorned with offerings to the spirits alongside Catholic iconography: pictures of the saints, a crucifix, etc. Rhythmic dancing and drumming send mediums into a trance through the night, and *encantados* (spirits) are invited to enter their bodies. Believers see the connection with the spirit world as a way of finding help in the world of the living: most lead extremely hard lives and face a daily struggle with poverty.

Another form of witchcraft, known as *Macumba*, is practiced in some quarters of Brazil. This black magic can be used for both good and evil. Make *encantados* angry, and you invite their menace into your life.

The menace of the *encantados* was never witnessed more powerfully than by the Ferreira family from Jabuticabal in 1965. The Catholic family was terrorized for five years by an entity so forceful that their eleven-year-old daughter was irrevocably altered by her experiences.

The family home was showered from inside and out with bricks, stones, and even eggs. Earthly causes were quickly ruled out, and the family sought outside intervention from their church and from a friend and neighbor, Joáo Volpe, who had an interest in the paranormal. Nothing helped rid the family of the poltergeist, but they could at least take some comfort in the knowledge that nobody had been injured by any of the bizarre events. Indeed, their daughter, Maria José Ferreira, seemed to be able to turn the activity to her own advantage and began to request that the entity shower her with objects she could actually enjoy. Soon, candy, flowers, fruit, and on one occasion, a piece of jewelry, appeared on demand.

There were dozens of witnesses to these paranormal events over the five years. Three visitors to the house described being "tapped on the head" by a stone, and compared the sensation to a "ball of compressed air." During a three-week period when the entity favored household objects, two other witnesses watched in disbelief as a bedroom mirror and a glass bowl from the kitchen made an elaborate air-born flights and switched rooms. Then, in March 1966, while Maria was surrounded by her friends in the lunchtime hustle and bustle of the school cafeteria, a small smoldering hole appeared on her clothes, as if from a cigarette burn. Within seconds, Maria was on fire.

It appeared that the *encantados* had decided playtime was over. In a chilling new chapter in the haunting, Maria became the victim of the spirit's increasing rage. The soles of her feet would be painfully pierced by needles, even if she wore shoes. On one occasion as many as fifty-five needles had to be removed. Maria became covered in lesions and bite marks, as day after day she was battered by her invisible assailant while the family watched powerlessly. No longer was she showered with gifts: heavy and dangerous household items began to be hurled at Maria. Lounge furniture and even a large gas cylinder were thrown at her with terrifying force.

The turning point for the desperate family and for the Volpes came when the *encantados'* attempts to end Maria's young life escalated. The sinister new attacks began to occur at night. As Maria lay sleeping, cups and bowls would be forcibly held to her mouth and nostrils, so that on several occasions she almost suffocated to death.

It could continue no longer. Desperate to help Maria, the Volpes took her to a spiritualist church, where a leading medium named Chico Xavier contacted an angry spirit who informed an astonished congregation that Maria's spirit had been a practicing black witch in a former life, and had harmed many people and caused the death of one. The poltergeist wanted to make her suffer in this life as it claimed she had made others do in a previous life.

Many prayers and rituals were carried out in a desperate attempt to rid her of the entity, but without success. The attacks continued until finally, in 1970, Maria drank a soda that had been mixed with a chemical poison and died instantly. She was just sixteen years old.

It is impossible to say whether it was the act of the *encantados* that ended her life, or whether it was an exhausted Maria herself, driven to despair by five years of madness and mayhem. All that can be said for certain is that when Maria José Ferreira died in 1970, the poltergeist attacks died with her. Whether her soul was that of a *Macumba* witch from a previous incarnation, or whether an honest Catholic teenager had been the victim of a malicious attack from beyond the grave, is a mystery that may never be solved.

The Carib Temple

AMAZON RAINFOREST, GUYANA

Guyana is a country of breathtaking natural beauty on the northeastern
tip of South America, but culturally and economically it has much in
common with the Caribbean islands that lie just off its coastline. The official
language is English, the most popular beverage is beer, and the radios play
reggae. The majority of Guyana's three-quarters-of-a-million people live
along the coast where belief in *jumbies* (ghosts) is widespread. Generations
of Guyanese have been raised listening to *jumbie* stories at night in their
backyards. Most feared of all were the "Dutchman jumbies," an echo of the
country's colonial past. These are evil spirits which attack people and break
the necks of small children. Many villages across Guyana still claim to be
haunted by at least one Dutchman jumbie, so that people dare not pass the
Dutch cemeteries at night.

The country's cultural heritage reaches much further back in history than
the arrival of the Dutch in the seventeenth century. The indigenous people
of Guyana are the Amerindians, the self-governing tribes of the Caribs and
the Arawaks, among others. Four-fifths of the country is unspoiled tropical
rainforest and has been home to these tribes for centuries. Until as late as the
nineteenth century, the Caribs and the Arawaks fought for dominance over
the coastal and central regions.

The Caribs particularly had a fearsome and war-like reputation. Columbus
encountered the Caribs and commented on the pride they took in scarring
their bodies by cutting their skin. The tribe was then known as the Galibi, a

name the Spanish corrupted to *Caníbal*. The ritual practices of Carib warriors then gave rise to the English word "cannibal."

Carib spirituality places great emphasis on the need for bravery. A valiant spirit, they believe, will spend eternity in the paradise of the "Fortunate Isles," served forever by Arawak slaves. The timid and the cowardly, however, are forced to serve the Arawaks for all eternity, in barren desert lands.

For a Carib, the death of an enemy was not enough to end the threat posed by the deceased: The spirit needed to be first released from the bones and flesh of the body, and then ingested into their own, transferring any powers and qualities it had to offer. This, then, was the reason behind the tribe's cannibalistic practices.

Once slain, the enemy's chest would be opened and the heart removed. The heart would be dried over the fire then ground until it became a fine powder. This powder would be mixed with a potent drink and ingested.

Many hundreds of these rituals took place in the deep heart of the rainforest in the hand carved granite temple of Canaima Yeng between A.D. 1600 and 1900. The body would be placed on a huge granite slab, like an outstretched palm, and the heart extracted. The stone fingers of the slab and the temple walls would have been awash with the blood of hundreds of victims.

Local tribes who still live in the region today have taken only a handful of trusted outsiders to see the temple. They tell of the mystical Carib sorcerer who last lived at the temple, and of the ethereal replaying of centuries of sacrifices that can be heard at night.

The brave few who have visited the temple and have camped near the site overnight are quick to substantiate these tales. At night, though the temple stands empty, the sound of a rhythmic drumbeat and spine-tingling chanting can be heard echoing through the pitch black of the rainforest. Worse still, an unearthly, ear-piercing scream silences the animals of the night. As the scream subsides, a momentary silence is swiftly followed by a new chant—a low, often broken, but nonetheless terrifying disembodied voice. Locals explain that the words of the chant echo those traditional to Carib human sacrifice rituals. Beneath the chant, and with the surrounding forest gripped by an unnatural stillness, is an unrelenting, rhythmic pounding on the drum.

The temple is now the destination of a small but growing number of so called ecotourists, keen to experience a more remote way of life. These intrepid few rarely remain overnight at the temple, but even by day feel distinctly uneasy at the site. An overwhelming sensation that they are being watched is often dismissed at the time as the product of an overactive imagination, fueled by gruesome tales from their guides about the horror of human sacrifice that ended so many lives. Others admit to a mildly uncomfortable pressure around their chest and a slight breathlessness. Again, most play down their symptoms.

Are these feelings entirely imagined? Is the uneasy aura simply the reso- nance of hundreds of human hearts ritualistically ripped from chests within the temple at Canaima Yeng? Or is there still within those walls a lingering malevolence from the spirit world that refuses to leave? Modern technological evidence points disturbingly to a sinister presence.

In 2002, two men from the U.S. camped at the temple site, and had their photographs taken at both entrances. When the photographs were developed, a perfect orb of light was clearly visible in each. Investigations ruled out technical faults or phenomena relating to the film or the camera. Chillingly, the orbs hovered in exactly the same position in each photograph: directly over the heart.

ICELAND

NORWAY

SWEDEN

FINLAND

RUSSIAN
FEDERATIO

ESTONIA

LATVIA

LITHUANIA

DENMARK

Castle of Ghosts

RUS.
FED.

BELARUS

Spedlins Tower

UNITED
KINGDOM

POLAND

REPUBLIC
OF
IRELAND

Leap
Castle

NETHERLANDS

The Lady
in Black

UKRAINE

Castle Coch

The Theatre Royal

GERMANY

The Tower
of London

BEL.

CZECH
REPUBLIC

SLOVAKIA

MOLDOVA

Underground City
of Death

AUSTRIA

HUNGARY

ROMANIA

FRANCE

SWITZ.

SLOVENIA

CROATIA

Island of Horror

BOSNIA-
HERZ.

SERBIA
&
MONTENEGRO

BULGARIA

ITALY

MAC.

PORTUGAL

SPAIN

ALBANIA

GREECE

TURI

House of Faces

Ntavelis's Cave

MOROCCO

TUNISIA

EG

ALGERIA

LIBYA

Europe

From the gothic bat-infested castles perched atop ancient rocks, to the palaces, churches, theaters, and hospitals of centuries-old cities, Europe is a continent steeped in history. It has witnessed hundreds of years of war and bloodshed, when brother fought brother and nation fought nation. Ancient sorrow and loss has not been forgotten and still revisits.

The Tower of London

With her 'ead tucked underneath her arm,
She walks the Bloody Tower
With her 'ead tucked underneath her arm
At the midnight hour.

This is part of a ghoulish song referring to Anne Boleyn, one of the most enduring ghosts of the bloody Tower of London. In 1536 her husband, Henry VIII, sentenced her to death after he grew tired of her inability to bear him a son. Her headless body haunts the White Tower and has terrified many a sentry out of his wits. In 1864, one such sentry spied the ghostly apparition—her head tucked under her arm—and challenged her with his bayonet. The weapon passed straight through her, causing the brave man to collapse in fear. A nineteenth-century account of an Anne Boleyn sighting by a guard reads as follows:

> *Slowly down the aisle moved a stately procession of Knights and Ladies, attired in ancient costumes; and in front walked an elegant female whose face was averted from him, but whose figure greatly resembled the one he had seen in reputed portraits of Anne Boleyn. After having repeatedly paced the chapel, the entire procession together with the light disappeared.* (Excerpt from *Ghostly Visitors* from "Spectre Stricken," London 1882.)

The dark walls of the Tower of London have borne witness to centuries of brutality and treachery. It is little wonder it has become the most foreboding building in Britain.

Commissioned by William the Conqueror in 1078 and completed almost twenty years later, the fortress represented a bastion of Norman power and towered ninety feet above the city. The White Tower has changed little from that time, but around twenty other towers and buildings from different periods in history have grown around it. Many of the towers held prison cells and torture chambers where numerous poor souls expired in misery.

Tower Green was reserved for Royal executions, while all other traitors were put to death on Tower Hill. Hundreds of executions were carried out here, their victims ranging from petty thieves to claimants to the throne.

Although often used as a royal residence, it was during the reign of Henry VIII that the Tower of London became regularly used as a prison. The Tower now boasts some of the most famous and unfortunate ghosts in British history.

The earliest recorded sighting of a ghost at the Tower was that of St. Thomas Becket in the thirteenth century. Thomas Becket was Chancellor of England (1155–1162) and Archbishop of Canterbury (1162–1170). His illustrious career ended following an argument with Henry II and his subsequent murder by the Knights of the court.

Sir Walter Raleigh, the famous seafaring explorer, was beheaded at the Tower in 1618. At his execution he asked to see the axe and observed, "This is a sharp medicine, but it is a physician for all diseases." His ghost makes an appearance now and again, wandering freely around the Tower as he did when he was imprisoned. Raleigh had not been as restricted in his movements as other prisoners. His ghost was last seen as recently as 1983 by a yeoman guard in the Byward Tower.

The bloody scene of the bungled execution of Lady Salisbury in 1541 is said to be re-enacted every year on the anniversary of her death. She refused to place her head on the executioner's block and was chased by the ax man, who eventually hacked her to death.

The Tower has played host to countless heinous acts but maybe none as tragic as the murders of two young "princes in the tower." Edward V, aged twelve, and Richard, Duke of York, aged ten, were imprisoned by their uncle, the Duke of Gloucester, who was plotting to become king. In 1483, soon after he was crowned King Richard III, the ghostly figures of the two young princes were seen gliding down the stairs of the Tower. Two hundred years later, workmen found a chest containing the skeletons of two young children, thought to be the dusty remains of the princes. They were given a royal burial and their ghosts were seen no more.

Perhaps one of the strangest apparitions to appear at the Tower was recorded by E. L. Swift, one-time keeper of the Crown Jewels in the nineteenth century. In 1817, he and his family were eating dinner in their rooms in the Martin Tower when his wife spotted something on the other side of the room. She screamed out in alarm and Swift turned around to see a cylindrical object filled with bubbling blue liquid floating towards them. He grabbed a chair and hurled it at the cylinder but it passed straight through the object, which then receded and disappeared.

The Tower of London is one of Britain's most important historical buildings. A thousand year history is imprisoned behind its portcullises and walls. Its rich, bloody history and brooding nature have fascinated and horrified count-less visitors.

The Theatre Royal

The Theatre Royal on Drury Lane is the oldest building in the world to have been in continual use as a theater, but its long history since 1663 has been checkered by fire, debt, and murder. It stood empty through the mid-1660s, as London was overcome first by plague and then by the Great Fire. When the theater reopened, King Charles II saw Nell Gwynn in her stage debut in 1665 and, famously, fell instantly in love with her. The Theatre Royal was ravaged by fire later that same year and again in 1809; it was attacked by an angry mob in 1737, and after sustaining further damage during another riot in 1780, it was guarded every night by troops until 1896. In 1800, the theater was even the setting for an assassination attempt when James Hadfield, freshly discharged from the army, attempted to shoot King George III as he sat in the royal box.

One of the most prominent eighteenth-century actors at the theater was an Irishman named Charles Macklin. His performance as Shylock in *The Merchant of Venice* in 1741 was monumental, as it marked the start of a new school of interpretive acting that was soon made famous by David Garrick. Great actor though he may have been (and a long-lived one at that: he is said to have died at the age of 107), Macklin was also a foul-tempered, violent man. During a petty argument in the green room over a wig, Macklin stabbed fellow actor Thomas Hallam through the eye with a sharp stick. Hallam died as a result of this injury, but Macklin escaped punishment, and his wraith has been trapped at the scene of his crime ever since. There have been sightings of a tall, thin ghost with a penitent, deeply lined and unattractive face, often in the orchestra pit in the early hours of the morning.

The most common sighting at the Drury Lane Theatre is of a rather grand, benevolent specter of an eighteenth-century gentleman wearing riding boots, a gray riding cloak, and the hilt of a sword at his waist. He is a sight most welcomed by casts of actors due to open with a new production. The Man in Grey, as he is known, has appeared to cast members of many successful productions at the theater over the years, but never before a flop, giving rise to many superstitions about him. (He appeared to every new cast of *Miss Saigon.*) Indeed, his association with roaring successes and long runs is so strong that when the theater was recently offered an exorcism, they politely declined.

On numerous occasions the slim, handsome figure has been spotted walking along the rows of the upper circle and around the theater before disappearing through a wall, or sitting in a particular seat in the upper circle, watching rehearsals. A cleaning lady reported seeing him sitting silently in the fourth row of the upper circle one morning at 10 A.M. in 1938; the following year, six psychic investigators saw him in the same seat. He is always silent. In 1939, he was seen by over fifty members of the cast of Ivor Novello's *The Dancing Years* as they posed on stage for a photo call, days before opening. Sightings are always between 10 A.M. and 4 P.M., making this a most unusual daytime haunting.

Although his identity in real life is uncertain, a gruesome discovery by workmen renovating the theater in the late nineteenth century puts our Man in Grey in a very different light. Behind the wall through which the ghost had walked during many sightings, the men discovered a long forgotten, sealed-off room. Inside lay a skeleton wearing the fragmented remains of what appeared to be eighteenth-century gray silk and satin. The dagger that had killed the man was still lodged in his rib cage.

Another ghostly presence has been reported by actors on stage at the theater. The 1940s actresses Betty Jo Jones and Doreen Duke, in separate productions, both claimed that their performances were enhanced as a result of feeling themselves "steered" into different positions on stage by invisible hands, and tugged skirts. Theater experts have speculated that this could be the influence of the great Joe Grimaldi, who gave his last performance on stage at the Theatre Royal and was renowned to be a very generous performer.

Another great British actor to have performed at the Theatre Royal was Dan Leno, who died in the early twentieth century. Leno had long suffered bladder problems and took to wearing lavender oil to help disguise the smell. Many actors have reported the smell of lavender suddenly pervading the air in backstage corridors. One actor, Stanley Lupino, exhausted after a performance and staying late in his dressing room, had the distinct feeling he was not alone and heard an invisible curtain being drawn. When he looked into his mirror to take off his make up, he saw the reflection of the famous Leno staring back at him. Only later did he discover he was using Leno's old dressing room.

Finally, and perhaps most dramatically of all, the theater was given a most regal visitation in 1948 when, during the run of *Oklahoma!*, Charles II himself, along with his royal entourage, appeared on stage. After more than 300 years in the business, the Theatre Royal, Drury Lane, continues to please its audiences, on both sides of the grave.

Castle Coch

W ith its lofty turrets, conical roofs, and enchanting medievalism, this truly breathtaking Victorian castle, nestled into the hillside outside Cardiff, seems to resonate with quiet romance and soft sanctuary. Take a tour of the inside and you will not be disappointed; the Victorian Gothicism of its interior heightens your sense that this is surely a perfect, tranquil haven. Delve into its most recent history, and the discovery that it was expertly redesigned in 1870 for the third Marquess of Bute will do nothing to shatter this illusion; the third Marquess of Bute, John Patrick Crichton-Stuart, was the richest man in the Victorian world.

But its peaceful appearance is an illusion. Castle Coch's history goes back far beyond its nineteenth-century restoration. Its thirteenth-century stone foundations have seen wars and warriors, intrigue, magic, and heartbreak.

By the late thirteenth century, the Normans, who had been waging war against the Welsh lords led by the charismatic Llewellyn ab Gruffydd, took control of Coch, and the Norman lord of Glamorgan, Gilbert de Clare, strengthened the castle.

This is the setting for our first spectral character. In keeping with the customs of the day, a noblewoman of the de Clare household in Coch at this time, named Matilda, was an active and enthusiastic huntswoman. Leading the hunt, she would tear through the forests surrounding the castle on horseback, in pursuit of wild boar, deer, or any other potential feast. She was renowned as a highly accomplished huntswoman and was deeply passionate about her

sport. Legend has it that on her deathbed she prayed to be permitted to spend eternity on the hunt through her beloved forest, rather than in heaven. It would seem she was granted her request. Locals have long reported hearing a large hunting party rampaging through the forests in the dead of night. Some sightings of the party have been seen, with a woman leading the hunt, giving rise to her name locally: *Mallt-y-Nos*, Matilda of the Night.

In the seventeenth century during the English Civil War, the neighboring Cardiff Castle was occupied by the Herberts, a great and powerful Royalist family. In fact, in the summer of 1645, King Charles I took shelter at Cardiff Castle. It was during this period that a cavalier, a member of the king's army, concealed a considerable hoard of loot in a subterranean room beneath the castle, no doubt with the intention of returning to collect the treasure when the war was settled. But fate dealt a different hand, and at the moment of his escape, a cannon exploded and he was killed. The Phantom Cavalier still haunts the castle today, locked in the search for all eternity.

Throughout the 200-year period before the Marquess of Bute's restoration of Coch in the nineteenth century, the castle lay abandoned and in ruins. The grounds were roamed freely by locals, who gathered food and hunted in the forests. It is here that we encounter the final phantom of Castle Coch: the ghost of Dame Griffiths.

Within the grounds of the castle is a dark, foreboding pool, said to be bottomless. Dame Griffiths had a young son who had set off alone into the forest, playing. Fearing he had been gone too long, Dame Griffiths went in search of her son and found evidence that he had fallen into the bottomless pool. His body was never recovered. The woman was so overcome that she never recovered and died soon after her son, heartbroken.

Today her ghost, a forlorn figure all in white, haunts the castle, pining for her son. Sightings of her are frequent. When the third Marquess of Bute died, his wife, Lady Bute, was said to have loved Castle Coch so dearly she decided to remain there. The constant appearance around the castle and forest of the hauntingly tragic figure of the woman in white proved too much for Lady Bute, however, and she later moved away altogether.

Will the ghost of Dame Griffiths ever rest, while the body of her beloved son lies in an unmarked watery grave?

Leap Castle

Visit Leap Castle today and you would be forgiven for thinking that the warm Irish hospitality you receive from the present owners, Sean Ryan and his family, reflects generations of close-knit, loving family occupants. The painstaking renovations, roaring fires, informal banquets, and beautiful music performed by Sean and his talented daughter, Ciara, may easily lull you into believing you are echoing centuries of happy times at Leap.

Don't be fooled.

Leap Castle, with its violent and bloody past, was known as Ireland's most haunted castle until the early 1990s. Indeed, its reputation for terrifying hauntings was so strong that locals had long avoided the place. Its gates stayed locked for over seventy years through the mid-twentieth century, and it fell into disrepair, finally standing as a dark and sinister shell.

The castle stands on an enormous rock, a strategic position in medieval times, guarding a pass through the Slieve Bloom Mountains. The site is reputedly druidic; certainly, pre-Christian artifacts have been uncovered there. It is also believed, by some archaeologists, to be resting upon an ancient ley line, as is so often the case at the site of multiple hauntings.

By the sixteenth century it had become the seat of the O'Carrolls, fierce and powerful Irish chieftains and the last big clan to hold out against the English in the seventeenth century. In 1532, the death of the head of the O'Carrolls gave rise to a leadership battle, murderous power-struggles, and treacherous betrayals. Two brothers were at the center of the struggle. The occasion of the final encounter between the two men is as chilling as it is infamous in local history.

One of the brothers, also the family priest, was saying mass in the chapel that formed part of the Great Tower. As he was kneeling in prayer at the altar, his brother and rival, Teige O'Carroll, known as "One-Eye," approached him from behind and plunged a dagger into his back. The priest fell prostrate across the altar and died in front of his family. Teige thereby worsened the already heinous crime of fratricide with the blasphemous murder of a priest during Holy Mass. The chapel has been known as the "Bloody Chapel" ever since.

The treachery of the clan goes far beyond this isolated incident, however. Stories of murder and torture abound, as with the O'Carroll chieftain who, mistrustful of his distant relatives, invited them to banquet with him at Leap, only to have them all murdered upon arrival.

Perhaps the most gruesome discovery was made at the turn of the twentieth century. It had long been known that in one corner of the tower was an *oubliette*, a room with a drop floor into which live prisoners were thrown. As the floor gave way, the unfortunate incarcerates faced two gruesome outcomes: either they would die an agonizing but fairly rapid death upon being impaled on a huge spike eight feet below the drop floor, or they would die a slow and torturous death of starvation, with the smells of the family's feasts assaulting them from the floors below. Escape from the *oubliette* was impossible, as became apparent when it was finally cleared out in the early 1900s and three full cartloads of skeletal remains were removed. It is not clear when the *oubliette* was last in use, although one of the workmen clearing it found a pocket watch from the 1840s.

The upright skeletons of three men were discovered later in the last century behind an internal wall of the main castle. (The then Lord Derby, who made the chilling discovery, immediately ordered the skeletons to be bricked up again, believing his ancestors must have had good reason to have put them there in the first place.) Yet more skeletal remains were discovered in myriad underground tunnels, in the dungeons, and hewn into the rock beneath the castle.

The ghostly sightings at Leap are numerous. Overnight guests at the castle often report a presence hovering at the foot of their bed. Others, staying in the state bedroom (always shunned by the Derbys' servants), report a tall female visitor in a red gown raising an ominous right hand above her head, as though to strike. Those who saw the lady in red would always report waking first feeling a cold terror in their chest. Peter Bartlett owned Leap Castle in the 1970s and claimed to have been plagued by poltergeist activity during renovations. The current owners, the Ryans, appear to be happy to live alongside the ghosts despite experiencing several freakish accidents during their renovation process. On one occasion Ryan had climbed a ladder to carry out some work, when it suddenly teetered backwards, as if pushed, and he was forced to leap several stories to the ground, shattering his ankles.

The most sinister presences have undoubtedly been centered on the Great Tower and the Bloody Chapel. During the long years when Leap Castle lay unoccupied, there were common sightings of the windows at the top of the tower suddenly being lit up with an intense light, equivalent to a whole room filled with candles. It was here that the most ferocious power of the "fire elemental" was unleashed at the end of the nineteenth century.

The Victorian inhabitants of the castle, Jonathan and Mildred Derby, followed the fashion for dabbling in the occult, with devastating consequences. In 1909, Mildred wrote an article about her experiences in the journal *Occult Review*:

*I was standing in the gallery looking down at the main floor, when I
felt somebody put a hand on my shoulder. The thing was about the
size of a sheep. Thin, gaunting, shadowy . . . its face was human, to
be more accurate inhuman. Its lust in its eyes which seemed half
decomposed in black cavities stared into mine. That horrible smell
one hundred times intensified came up into my face, giving me a
deadly nausea. It was the smell of a decomposing corpse.*

The malevolent "fire elemental," half-man, half-beast, with rotting eyes and
smelling of sulfur and dead flesh, wreaked havoc well into the twentieth
century in the Great Tower at Leap. Brave souls who dared investigate the
abandoned castle claimed to have felt the cold chill of terror and heard
unearthly sniffling noises accompanied by a putrid smell. A series of masses
were said at the site, and visits were made by numerous psychics, until finally,
in the 1970s, Peter Bartlett brought in a Mexican white witch to exorcise the
castle. After hours in the Bloody Chapel, she declared that the spirits did not
wish to leave, but were no longer malevolent.

Today, the Ryan family seems happy that the spirits who share their home are
no longer a sinister presence. They will tell of ghostly shadows, the occasional
touch and feel of a spirit as it brushes past. They welcome visitors, some of
whom claim to have seen the dominant spirit in Leap Castle today, that of the
slaughtered priest in the Bloody Chapel. But the ghostbusters who visit them,
all eagerly hoping to catch spectral images on film, often leave disappointed,
for as soon as they set foot inside the chapel, they find their camera shutters
have locked.

Spedlins Tower

TEMPLAND, DUMFRIES AND GALLOWAY, SCOTLAND

This is the story of a man whose incarceration, starvation, and death (the direct result of another's act of inhumanity) only now can be fully appreciated as the heartbreaking tragedy it really was. Today, more than 350 years later, surviving members of two Scottish clans, scattered on both sides of the Atlantic Ocean, are still working to lay his ghost to rest.

Dunty Porteous was a miller who supplied bread to his community in the estates of the Jardine family of Dumfries and Galloway, whose seat was at Spedlins Tower. He was an honest and hardworking man who was unjustly blamed for a mill fire in 1650 by the laird and patriarch of the clan, Sir Alexander Jardine. Jardine had Dunty chained by his ankles and wrists to the walls of the dungeons beneath Spedlins Tower, while awaiting his trial.

Immediately after Dunty's incarceration, the laird was called away on business to Edinburgh and rode off immediately with his entourage and the only key to the dungeon. By the time he discovered his fatal mistake, he had been away for some time and still had to make the long ride back to Spedlins. The fear of what he would face upon arrival must have haunted him throughout that journey, though it could not have prepared him for the gruesome sight that awaited his return.

Dunty's cell was accessible both by a heavy wooden door and by a small, square trapdoor. It was a windowless room. Chained to the wall, with solid wood and thick stone walls separating him from the rest of the castle, he would have had no means of making his presence heard and certainly no hope

of escape. He had been left alone in the dark, dank, airless space for weeks. No one had fed him. No one had given him water. Few knew of his presence there; those who did were miles away and had taken with them his only means of salvation. Death from starvation is a slow, torturous process, and the survival instinct drives a man to desperate measures.

Jardine arrived back at the castle and headed straight for the dungeons. Unlocking the door he would have been confronted first by the stench of rotting flesh. Braving a closer inspection, the laird was sickened to see that in his last desperate days, fighting for his life, Dunty Porteous had gnawed the flesh from his own hand and foot.

The family had Dunty's body buried and hoped that would ease his spirit to rest in peace. But Dunty's spirit was not at peace, and had no intention of being laid to rest. Immediately after the funeral, the family began to be plagued by a poltergeist wailing and calling for food day and night. The family, sleep-deprived and tormented with fear, sought the help of priests, who attempted to exorcise the spirit. They failed to free Spedlins Tower from Dunty's ghost, but succeeded in "grounding" it, confining it to the dungeon in which Dunty's suffering had taken place, by attaching the spirit of the miller to a large, black, leather-bound bible that the family then placed in a stone alcove in the dungeon. The main house was freed from the spirit of Dunty the miller, but the family seat was not. The screaming continued night after night, along with sounds of "flutterings" against the dungeon door, as the spirit tried to break free. It is said that if a twig was pushed through the keyhole, it would be pushed back, gnawed, and stripped of its bark. This legend survives to this day, and locals tell of this phenomenon occurring in living memory.

By the nineteenth century, the descendants of Alexander had tired of sharing their home with the persistent spirit of Dunty Porteous and moved across the river Annan to a new, more spacious mansion house, known as Jardine Hall. But the haunting continued.

Today Jardine Hall has been razed to the ground by the modern descendants of the Jardine clan, and Spedlins Tower has been renovated and restored by its new owners. Before its renovation, the tower stood empty, a semi-ruin, but locals still reported hearing screams and moans from within its dungeons. There were several sightings of a tall, wan figure, his face wracked with pain. In every sighting, the wraith was missing a hand. Upon the sale of Spedlins Tower to a family outside the clan, the spirit seems to have shifted its emphasis again, and the focus of its activities became the new home of the chief clansman, Sir Alexander. It was clear the spirit of Dunty would not rest until its deathly cries were heeded.

In 1998, the February issue of *The Scottish Journal* shed new light on this story. Lady Mary Jardine Applegirth, the wife of the chief Jardine clansman, wrote an article in which she revealed that research had uncovered the story of a maid at Spedlins Tower in the early seventeenth century who was raped by the Laird Alexander and consequently gave birth to a son. The maid was a Porteous; her son was Dunty. The Dunty Porteous incarceration was suddenly revealed to be a far greater crime: Laird Alexander had brought about the death of his own illegitimate son.

The Jardine clan motto, *Cave asdum* (Beware I am here), now seems all the more sinister; rightfully, it should have been Dunty's own motto. So wrongfully denied it in life, it seems he vowed to adopt the motto in death, ensuring that generations of the Jardine clan could not forget his presence, as his own father had done.

The modern branches of the Jardine clan have since met with those of the Porteous family, and have had Dunty, his family, and their descendants legally written into their own family tree. Together they held a ceremony at Spedlins Tower, commemorated Dunty Porteous, and planted a tree in his honor. They sincerely hope this will finally allow his spirit to rest in peace.

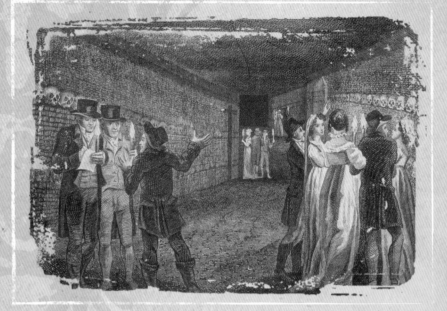

Underground City of Death

PARIS, FRANCE

Strolling along the wide chic streets of Paris, marveling at the wonderful mellowness of the buildings, you would be shocked to learn that beneath your feet lay the brittle skeletons of over seven million Parisians. Stolen from their graves, these disturbed souls now slumber uneasily in the dark, damp tunnels that spread like tentacles beneath the City of Romance.

The tunnels are known as the catacombs or the Empire of Death, and all visitors are disquieted by their ghastly contents. The Empire of Death is a network of tunnels and caves that run for almost 180 miles beneath the city. They date back to Roman times, when limestone was quarried to begin building the Paris we know today. The quarries provided centuries of building materials until the threat of collapse forced them to be abandoned.

During the eighteenth century the cemeteries of Paris were suffering from a crisis of overcrowding. The graveyards were so full that bodies were buried one on top of the other, and mass graves were created to help ease the problem. The grounds within the graveyards rose higher and higher, in some cases reaching more than twenty feet above the road. Eventually the cemetery walls began to collapse, spilling decayed corpses out onto the pavements. Putrid liquids oozed down the streets, spreading death and disease, and the air was filled with the repugnant smell of rotting flesh.

A solution had to be found, and in 1785 a decision was made to empty the cemeteries and move the bones into the catacombs. Disturbing the dead is not a task to be undertaken lightly. Pity the workers who loaded the carts in the sickly light of dawn and made the eerie procession to the mouth of the catacombs every day for two years.

Initially, three million bodies were moved, the combined dead of four hundred years. How the emptied graveyards would have echoed in their absence. The movement of bones continued sporadically for at least seven decades, and the catacombs now hold the remains of at least seven million people.

The mountains of bones were not dumped haphazardly, but were built into the most ghoulish of walls. Femurs were piled onto femurs and tibias stacked in neat rows. Skulls were built into columns and formed into intricate patterns of hearts and crosses. The walls are deep and about four feet high. They run for miles along the length of the tunnels.

Part of the catacombs is now open to the public so the stout of heart can view the wall of death and stare into the black eyes of the empty skulls. Down in the darkness of the tunnels it is utterly silent save for the drip of oily water falling from the ceilings. The cold and damp hugs your chest, causing you to shiver involuntarily. There is the prevailing sense of the passage of time, the tunnels having borne witness to important events throughout history.

In 1847, the members of the Paris orchestra descended into the gloom to perform a clandestine recital. The author Balzac is said to have escaped his creditors by hiding out in the tunnels. During the Second World War partisans hid in the deep recesses of the caves, and prostitutes chased from the streets conducted their business against the seeping walls.

The catacombs exert a morbid fascination over the citizens of Paris. They have become the haunt of a group of people known as *cataphiles*. These lovers of the netherworld hunt out secret entrances to the catacombs and explore the miles upon miles of uncharted tunnels. It has been known for the tunnels to swallow these foolhardy adventurers and never to spit them out.

In 1961, a young Parisian named Henry discovered a hidden entrance to the catacombs, and along with six of his friends he went deep underground to explore the unknown. After walking through the dust of centuries for a couple of hours, the group's lamps and torches suddenly failed. They were plunged into utter darkness knowing there was nothing worse, for when the lights go out it was said the tunnels change and move.

The group huddled together and prayed hard. Suddenly, Henry's torch flickered back on and they heaved a collective sigh of relief. As Henry knew the tunnels better than anyone, the group held hands with Henry leading the way. All the way back to the surface Henry could feel his friend Louis gripping his hand hard. As he approached the entrance, Henry turned to his friends with a whoop of triumph. His whoop turned to a scream of terror when he saw they were not there; only a black shadow which left his hand and drifted back down the tunnel. He never saw his friends again.

A more recent story concerns a young female "cataphile" who became separated from her friends while exploring the tunnels. She had seen a light glimmering in the distance and had followed it thinking someone was lost. The light always moved ahead of her, no matter how fast she went. She began to call for her friends to help, but could only hear her own cries echoing back. She ran faster until she eventually came to a dead-end where the most gruesome sight met her eyes. Propped against the wall was a skeleton in ragged clothes wearing modern-day trainers. The young girl turned and ran, blind with terror, a dark shadow following her through the twists and turns of the tunnels. She was lucky and managed to find her way out. She was later found huddled in the corner of a café, smeared in blood and dust with a vacant stare in her eyes.

A multitude of angry spirits roam the winding tunnels, seeking someone or something to blame. The catacombs are no respecter of peace, and it would be impossible for these civilians of the past to rest while crushed and crammed, suffocating amongst another's bones. There are noblemen's bones intermingled with those of peasants and generations of families separated in death as they were not in life.

Many people are gripped by a sharp terror when descending the spiral staircase that leads to the main bone depository. They hear voices and whispers and muffled cries of anguish, maybe the souls of mothers searching through the piles of bones for their infants so cruelly ripped from their arms. Their bones, meant to rest together, are now scattered far and wide.

Cameras and camcorders often stop working, or if a picture is developed it is usually filled with odd mists and lights. With the clamor of modern-day Paris rattling above their heads and the unwelcome arrival of tourists, is it any wonder the generations of deceased wish to vent their indignation?

Ntavelis's Cave

MOUNT PENTELI, NEAR ATHENS, GREECE

About nine miles from the center of Athens, in Mount Penteli, is a huge cave connecting a series of subterranean tunnels. It is a site that exudes a powerful aura and that has been the focus of intrigue and paranormal phenomena since earliest recorded history. Not surprisingly, it has also been the site of many places of worship through the centuries.

Follow one particular tunnel and you are led into a colossal underground chamber, with a small pool and an ancient temple to the primitive New Stone Age Greek god, Pan, the half-man and half-goat protector of shepherds.

In the nineteenth century, the infamous highwayman thief, Ntavelis (also spelled Davelis), used the caves as a hideout for his band of seventy men. Together, they committed many atrocities against local villagers, commonly dipping their victims' feet in boiling oil until given the information they sought. In one much told story, Ntavelis kidnapped a child, a young girl, and left her tied on Mount Penteli, displayed for her family to see she was still alive, while they frantically tried to raise the ransom. Indeed kidnapping, particularly of children, provided Ntavelis's staple income. Ntavelis was ultimately killed by a group of vigilantes from a village near Delphi. Subsequently, his name was forever linked to the caves.

Today, the rituals of both New Age and Satanist covens are evident in the cave. Strange symbols adorn the walls, and periodically victims of animal sacrifice are found at the entrance to the cave or surrounding tunnels. It seems the aura of the cave has changed and now attracts an altogether more sinister presence.

Throughout its history, locals told of strange orbs of light, ghostly apparitions, hazy green mists, and strange, sheep-like creatures with piercing luminous eyes. In the 1960s and 1970s, paranormal investigators at the cave began to report a variety of new phenomena. A lot of what they experienced there involved strange electrical faults—lights surging, even without battery power; cameras refusing to operate in certain areas of the cave; and photographs where faces were covered by a green haze; or, most bizarrely, where the camera and hands appeared in the photo, almost as if the eyes of the photographer had taken the picture. Tourists reported photographs where they saw themselves twice: their actual bodies and a representation of themselves apparently "carved" into the rock formations behind them.

At this point, the caves were sealed off to the public, as they became the focus of a frantic top secret NATO project, involving the blasting of new tunnels through the rock. Then, as suddenly as it had begun, all military operations at the site were abandoned. Machinery remained uncollected. New tunnels led merely to dead ends; old tunnels stood filled in, apparently pointlessly. NATO's purpose at the site has never been established. (What is known is that many of the workers involved in the project have since died of cancer, and that, coincidentally, many boxes of abandoned anti-cancer drugs were found in the cave after the troops moved out.) But the paranormal phenomena continued, and the investigators moved back in.

New mysteries began to be uncovered. A child's footprints were found, imprinted into a concrete floor—while it was still wet—that had been laid by military personnel in one of the new tunnels. The footprints showed that a barefoot child had walked up to a dead end where the rock had not been blasted, but did not walk back again, as if the child had either vanished into thin air or walked through the wall. A strange doll was seen hanging against the mountainside, at such an inaccessible spot that a member of the army's special forces was the only person able to reach it, though not without considerable effort. Overnight, a replica doll was seen in exactly the same spot.

Who, or what, had gone to such extreme lengths to place the unearthly doll in such a spot was never established. Rumors of dark, shadowy forms also began filtering through.

The road that accesses the area of the cave has also been the subject of many strange occurrences. At one point the road clearly appears to be at an incline, and yet there are many reports of cars stalling and rolling *uphill*. The strangest of these reports is of an abandoned vehicle that (judging by track marks in the snow) appeared to have traveled across a steep, near vertical incline of rough, rocky terrain without any apparent damage to the undercarriage. Scientific investigations at the site and inside the cave indicate highly irregular electro-magnetic readings and a degree of anti-gravitational energy.

Even more disturbing were accounts of the bizarre and inexplicable behavior of some of the investigators themselves. Many of them wandered out of the cave dazed and confused, claiming to have experienced "lost time" and panic attacks; and there have even been rumors that some investigators failed to return at all. Inexplicable phenomena continue to be reported at Ntavelis's Cave. What unearthly entities are at force there remains a mystery.

Castle of Ghosts

D ragsholm Slot castle in Sealand, Denmark, is home to three prominent ghosts and a whole host of lesser spirits. Part of the castle has been converted into a hotel, but guests are not necessarily granted a good night's sleep.

The White Lady is the most frequently occurring apparition and has been seen pacing the corridors and weeping on many occasions. It is said that she was the daughter of one of the noble families who once resided here. When young, she fell in love with a commoner who worked at the castle. Her father would have been incensed at the union, so the affair was conducted in secret. They became careless, however, as young lovers do, and one fateful day her father caught them in an embrace. His fury knew no bounds, and he ordered his daughter to be imprisoned within the thick walls of the castle.

During the 1930s, a new toilet block was being installed that required old walls to be torn down. Behind one such wall workers found the ancient skeleton of a woman wearing a white dress. Could this indeed be the remains of the lovelorn maiden condemned to haunt the castle forever, weeping for her lost love and life?

A friend of the present owners has another tale to tell of the White Lady of Dragsholm. During the winter of 1993, a female guest was sleeping in the royal suite. Her granddaughter was asleep in the adjoining dining room, and the door between the two rooms was left open. At about three in the morning the woman woke up and was aware of a strange feeling of being watched. She noticed a tall lady wearing white standing at the open doorway between

the two rooms. The lady was standing with her arms folded tightly across her chest, and the granddaughter could be seen quite clearly through the translucent folds of her gown. The female guest was not of a timid persuasion and inched her way slowly out of bed to take a closer look. As her feet touched the ground the lady in white disappeared "like a soap bubble."

A psychic invited to take part in a film being made at the castle also sensed something in the royal suite. She felt that a baby had been born in the room and saw the same lady dressed in white standing with her arms folded in the doorway. The lady in white was the child's nurse, and she was forbidding anyone but family from entering the room.

A much less stern spirit is that of the Gray Lady. She is said to be the ghost of a maid who once worked at the castle. She suffered for years from a terrible toothache that was eventually cured, allowing her to live the rest of her days comfortably. As gratitude for her cure, she patrols the castle corridors checking that all is in order. She leaves in her wake a sense of well-being and peace.

Perhaps the most renowned of all the castles specters is that of James Hepburn, fourth Earl of Bothwell who was incarcerated in Dragsholm castle in the 1570s, where he was chained to a post and kept in the dank darkness for five years. He was driven insane and eventually died in the cellar in 1578. The semicircular groove caused by years of his pacing can still be seen, worn into the cellar floor.

The insane cries of the Earl can still be heard, muffled by the thick castle walls, and the sounds of hooves on cobbles and the screeching of carriage wheels can be heard time and again in the empty courtyard. Is it the Earl, doomed to be brought again and again to the scene of his death?

House of Faces

There is a small inauspicious house on a back street in the Spanish town of Bélmez de la Moraleda that contains living proof that not all things in this world are as they should be.

On a sunny morning in August 1971, María Gómez Pereira came into her kitchen to cook the family breakfast and noticed a strange mark on the kitchen hearth. A scrupulously house-proud woman, María scrubbed and scrubbed at the mark but could not remove it. The mark grew bigger over the next few days, and María grew increasingly frustrated. As the mark increased in size, it seemed to evolve into a face that stared out at María from the cold concrete floor. At first María blamed her fanciful imagination; maybe it was the way the sun shone through the windows, playing with the shadows on the floor. She called to her husband, Juan, and son, Miguel, to dismiss her concerns, but to her great consternation they both admitted that they, too, could see the face on the floor. The face began to change, taking on a sad and mournful expression, and when repeated attempts to clean it off failed, the family fled to a neighbor's house in fear.

During the following days, friends and relations came to view the haunted hearth and all agreed on the presence of the unearthly visage. Miguel became considerably disturbed by the image and one day took a pickaxe and smashed the hearth to pieces. The chunks of cement were removed and a new floor lain in its place.

The Pereira family was confident they had rid themselves of the unsettling phenomena and moved back into their home. Imagine their horror and dismay when, a week later, the face reappeared on the hearth once more. The face refused to be erased and the story spread throughout Bélmez. The Pereira household became the focus of enormous public interest, and the face was christened the *Pava*. The city council became involved and offered to carry out an investigation into the cause of the eerie sensation. A pit was dug beneath the hearth, three yards deep and one-and-a-half yards wide. To everyone's surprise the excavation revealed a collection of ancient human bones and a pair of headless skeletons.

The Pereira house had been built on land that once formed part of the cemetery of the local Catholic church. The cemetery was ancient, dating back to Roman times, and was the resting place for a mixed bag of religious souls. The church had been subjected to major restoration works just days before the manifestation of the *Pava*. The upheaval resulted in some graves being exhumed and moved elsewhere.

The bones found under the Pereira hearth were taken away for analysis. They were found to be adolescent bones dating back to the thirteenth century, and were later transferred to a Catholic church for reburial. It was hoped that the discovery and reburial of the bones would appease any latent spirits and spell an end to the persistent *Pava*. The hearth was once more repaired and the Pereira family resumed their once peaceful existence.

However, the *Pava* was not to be defeated and it once more manifested itself upon the hearth along with a collection of new faces which began to appear all across the kitchen floor. They were young, old, male, and female, all conveying a myriad of emotions that faded, then grew in radiance. The faces would not be scrubbed away and were heedless of Miguel's pickaxe.

The local authorities had consulted so-called experts on paranormal phenomena, but received no satisfactory answers to the many questions surrounding the haunted floor. The huge crowds being drawn to the Pereira house were having a disruptive influence on the community, so the authorities decided to call in outside help to prove that the phenomenon was a hoax.

Professor German de Argumosa, a leading parapsychologist, arrived in Bélmez in 1972, along with a host of other experts in related fields. What they found prompted one of them, Professor Hans Bender, to state, "Without doubt this is the most important paranormal phenomenon of the century." They were utterly amazed at what they saw. The faces on the floor moved and shifted while they were watching. The expressions on the faces changed continually from one emotion to another, some features dissolving into the concrete floor, while others rose vividly to take their place.

Thousands of people witnessed the sensational apparitions, from ordinary individuals to leading church officials and prominent members of society. They all left the house shaken to the core, their lives significantly changed by the experience.

In the presence of a television crew and hundreds of witnesses, Professor Argumosa divided the kitchen floor into sections, photographing each one before covering and sealing the floor. Then, witnessed by the town notary, the room, its windows, and the door were sealed with wax.

After three months had passed the room was opened, and the faces were found to have moved and changed position. The experiment was declared a success and the possibility of the faces having been hoaxed could now be definitively ruled out. The scientists continued to search for an explanation and every test known was applied to the faces. X-rays, acoustic tests, and infra-red and ultraviolet analysis all were carried out. There were tests to detect radioactivity and organic and chemical composites. Nothing was discovered, and there was no evidence whatsoever of paints or dyes in the cement. In short, no scientific explanation for the phenomenon was found.

Many people believed that the images were triggered by psychokinetic energy emitted from María Pereira, as the expressions on the faces seemed to mirror her emotions, and as María aged, the faces lost their vivacity. María died on February 3, 2004, at age 85, and contrary to all expectations, the faces have continued to flourish on her old kitchen floor.

Are we ready to believe that the audacious souls once buried under that hearth have indeed found a way to connect with our world? Experts are no closer to discovering the truth behind the faces of Bélmez than they were three decades ago. It is the most astounding confirmation of the existence of mysteries that reach beyond all human comprehension.

The Lady in Black

The Polish city of Krakow is steeped in ghostly legends. There are spirits bleeding out of the ancient stone walls and flitting silently through the dark and narrow alleyways.

Wawel Hill is at the center of the city and is home to the royal castle and Wawel Cathedral. Many kings have been crowned here and buried in the vaults under the cathedral. According to legend, all the dead kings of Poland gather together on Christmas Eve in these underground vaults. The vaults are certainly eerie, with dark shadows floating across the rooms and extraordinarily unearthly music coming from empty tombs.

There is a network of caves beneath Wawel Hill where centuries of folklore, legend, and the unexplained mingle in an uneasy truce. It is said that old King Kazimir discovered a secret passage leading into the hill and found his way into a chamber lit by a strange and pulsating stone. This is said to provide Krakow with its mystical energy. The Dragon's Lair is the most famous of these caves and is said to have once housed a terrible monster. Its entrance is now guarded by a tame stone dragon, but a hideous atmosphere still pervades the furthest corners of its dark interior.

One of the more friendly ghosts of Krakow is that of jester Stanczuk. He was court jester to old King Sigismund and a great patriot. Whenever Poland is in danger, he is seen dancing on the battlements of the castle, and his bells can be heard tinkling across the city.

North of Wawel Hill, in All Saints Place, is a mansion that now houses the mayor's office. The forlorn figure of a woman in black is often seen wandering the building wringing her hands in grief or loitering aimlessly in and out of the shadows of the square.

The melancholy spirit is that of a young woman called Miss Wielopolska who once lived in the mansion with her monster of a father. She had the misfortune to fall in love with a young man well below her in social standing. Her father could not abide the shame the relationship brought upon the family and decided that the death of his daughter would be much easier to bear. He imprisoned Miss Wielopolska in her bedroom and announced that she had moved abroad. The wickedly calculating man instructed a trusted servant to go and fetch a certain young and inexperienced priest to the house. On a dark and sullen night, the unfortunate priest was kidnapped from his rooms, blindfolded, and thrown into the back of a blacked-out carriage. He was warned to ask no questions, and told that if he agreed to listen to a dying girl's last confession, then he would be delivered safely home. He was taken to Miss Wielopolska's bedroom, and only then was the blindfold taken off. He listened in silence to the poor girl's confession, and as her last words evaporated into the perfumed air of her room, a masked figure swathed in cloaks stepped out from behind the curtains and sliced off her head with a single swipe of a sword.

The priest had barely time to scream before he was hauled out of the room and taken downstairs. He was handed a cup of suspicious looking liquid, and told to drink it as it would help to calm his shattered nerves. He did not swallow it, but managed to pour the liquid down the inside of his clerical robes while his captor was distracted.

He was once again blindfolded, bundled into the carriage, and taken home. On arriving back in his rooms, he was horrified to discover that his body was covered in burns and blisters where the poison liquid had soaked through to his skin.

It wasn't until many years later that the priest was unwittingly called once more to the mansion. This time he arrived in daylight and at once recognized the place as being the scene of the hideous murder he had witnessed and had never been able to forget. He gave evidence against the monstrous father who was convicted of murder and sentenced to death.

Miss Wielopolska was unable to forgive or forget and now hovers in a place that is neither before nor after.

Island of Horror

Poveglia is a small island floating in the lagoons of Venice. In stark contrast to the beauty of its surroundings, the island is a festering blemish. The waves reluctantly lapping its darkened shores will often carry away the polished remains of human bones.

When the first outbreak of bubonic plague swept through Europe, the number of dead and dying in the city of Venice became unbearable. The bodies were piling up, the stench was oppressive, and something had to be done. The local authorities decided to use Poveglia as a dumping ground for the diseased bodies. The dead were hauled to the island and dumped in large pits or burned on huge bonfires. As the plague tightened its grip, people panicked, and those showing the slightest symptoms of the Black Death were dragged screaming from their homes. These living victims, including children and babies, were taken to the island and thrown into the pits of rotting corpses, where they were left to die in agony. As many as 160,000 tormented bodies were disposed of over the years.

The soil on the island, combined with the charred remains of some of the bodies, formed a layer of sticky ash on the land. The top layer of ash has dried in the sun to form a fine dust that swirls in the breeze and catches in lungs. Part of the island core consists of a layer of human remains. Fishermen avoid this area, as the chances of catching a body part are quite high.

In 1922, a psychiatric hospital was built. It was an imposing building with a magnificent bell tower. The patients immediately reported seeing the ghosts

of rotting plague victims and of hearing whispers echoing off the walls. Their harrowing reports were dismissed; they were already deemed mad.

The hospital was run by a doctor who was a little too ambitious. He decided to make a name for himself by experimenting on his patients in a bid to discover the cause of their insanity. His methods were crude, to say the least. Loboto-

mies were performed using a basic hand drill or just a hammer and chisel. The already deluded patients were taken to the observation tower, where they were subjected to the most hideous of tortures.

After years of performing these unholy acts, the doctor himself began seeing the ghosts of harrowed plague victims. It is said they led him to the bell tower, where he threw himself off. Miraculously he did not die immediately, but according to a nurse, as he lay writhing in agony, a fine mist swirled up around him, entered his body, and choked him to death. It is rumored that he is bricked up in the bell tower, and on a still night the bell can be heard tolling across the bay.

The hospital has since closed down, and the island is uninhabited. It is not open to tourists, and its ashy beaches remain deserted. A family recently sought permission to visit the island, hoping to buy it cheaply and build a holiday home. They left before the night was out and have refused to comment on the reason for their abrupt departure. The only fact known is that their daughter's face was ripped open by "something" and needed fourteen stitches.

A few people have dodged the light police patrol that guards the island, and all have sworn never to return. They say the moans and screams that reverberate around the island are unbearable. There is a feeling of the most intense evil, and one misguided thrill-seeker, upon entering the deserted hospital, was told, "Leave immediately and do not return."

PHILIPPINES

I N D O N E S I A

PAPUA
NEW GUINEA

SOLOMON
ISLANDS

EAST TIMOR

VANUATU

A U S T R A L I A

The Street with No Name

Monte Cristo

The Mayanup
Poltergeist

Hell on Earth

NEW
ZEALAND

Australia

When the harmony of the lives of the indigenous peoples was shattered by an influx of Europeans in the nineteenth century, the psyche of an entire continent was irrevocably changed. From the vast expanses of the outback to the horrors of the Victorian prisons, Australia is rich in the spectral echoes of times past.

Hell on Earth

Port Arthur, on the Tasman peninsula off the coast of mainland Australia, boasts some of nature's finest fortifications. The tallest stretch of coastal cliffs in Australia, the blistering seas, and the dark, colossal forests provide an imposing backdrop for one of the nineteenth century's most infamous prisons. The location, the conditions, and the knowledge that inmates had scant hope of ever returning home, earned the prison its nickname of "Hell on Earth."

For modern Australians, the name "Port Arthur" remains synonymous with misery, inhumanity, and death. In the nineteenth century, thousands of criminals (many of them guilty only of petty theft, and many of them women and children) were shipped from Britain to Australia in the dreaded punishment known as "transportation." The journey itself was a harrowing 15,000 miles and could take up to eight months; many didn't survive. In 1830, the penal settlement on the mainland began to rid itself of its worst male offenders, and a shipload arrived on the island known then as Van Dieman's Land to be put to work on a timber station supplying the Australian government. By 1833, Port Arthur had become an established prison settlement.

The penitentiary operated for forty-four years, during which time 13,000 men were incarcerated within its walls. As soon as they were off the ship, the men were set to work—backbreaking logging or stone breaking for hours every day made all the more dangerous by the weighty chains they wore around their ankles. Punishments for slackers were harsh, and lengthy public lashings with a "cat-o'-nine-tails" were commonplace. Gradually a new style of punishment was incorporated into the prison regime: men were subjected to

months, sometimes years, of solitary confinement. Confinement meant being restricted in specially designed cells known as "'dark" or "'dumb" cells, which were entered via a series of doors designed to exclude all outside noise and light. The punishments and the monotonous work drove many men insane, and one man stands out above all others as its chief architect. In 1833 Charles Booth, the commandant of the settlement, vowed that he would take "the vengeance of the Law to the utmost limits of human endurance," and he certainly achieved his goal. Indeed the convicts themselves felt Booth's regime went far beyond testing the boundaries of "human endurance." Asked to describe the impact of the Port Arthur penal settlement, one ex-convict simply said that it "broke men's spirits."

Today there is little doubt that the spirits of many hundreds of men who died there were, indeed, broken. Visitors to the site leave with one lasting impression: an uneasy sense of the despair that filled the prison. Paranormal activity is extensive and is thoroughly logged; visitors are asked to complete an "unusual occurrence" form, to keep a record of any experiences that occur and their precise location. Todd Darling, a regular tour guide at Port Arthur, has been struck by the similarities between all these reports, remarking that visitors to the site consistently file reports describing the same things and places as reports filed by strangers ten years earlier.

Many of the stories describe floating orbs of light and sudden cold spots, accompanied by overwhelming feelings of hatred and anger. Hearing voices or footsteps is common. Some reports describe apparitions of officers or convicts, and more rarely, some claim to have had conversations with a convict who suddenly vanishes.

Spectral activity not apparent to the naked eye has been captured on camera or film with alarming frequency at Port Arthur. In one case, a woman was filmed by her husband using night vision during one of the after-dark, lantern-lit ghost tours of the site. When they watched the footage the next day, it clearly showed a glowing ethereal cloud pass through her body and leave the room, closely followed by a loud bang that made all members of the party shout out in terror. Her husband had seen nothing of this through his lens as he had been filming.

The most sinister reports are from people who have experienced more direct spectral contact. One of the cellblocks on the site is filled with a particularly overwhelming sense of foreboding. The atmosphere is so menacing that many visitors who enter its thick, cold stone walls have the distinct feeling that they are being watched. Some are overcome with the sense of utter misery that seems to reside there, as well as the odd sensation that they are lost (in fact, a few find themselves literally lost, and have to seek help to find their way out of the block). The most disturbing incidents involve one particular cell in which some visitors have reported suddenly finding themselves unable to move and fighting for breath, feeling their throats constrict, as if gripped by spectral hands. In some cases the "attack" leaves thumbprint-like bruising on their necks. One woman reported feeling consumed with despair that she would never be able to leave.

There is a small island in the bay at Port Arthur known as the Island of the Dead. It is a cemetery where more than a thousand souls lay buried. Death would surely have come as a blessed release for many of them. But the question remains: Just how many did find such release, and how many remain trapped to this day, in their "Hell on Earth"?

Monte Cristo

JUNEE, NEW SOUTH WALES

Just off the Hume highway in New South Wales, a short distance from Wagga Wagga, is the quaint and sleepy town of Junee. Drive through the peaceful streets, and you will be stopped in your tracks by the sight of an imposing mansion house squatting high on a hill and casting its gloomy shadow down on to the town and its residents.

This is the infamous Monte Cristo, Australia's "most haunted house." Over countless years, this dark and brooding homestead has been plagued by a catalogue of ghastly incidents and horrific deaths. At least seven ghoulish residents are reputed to be at large in both the house and the grounds.

Monte Cristo, meaning "Mount of Christ," was built in 1884 by Christopher William Crawley, a local farmer whose luck changed when he acquired some land under provision of the Robertson's Act of 1861. He was married to Elizabeth, a hard and brutal woman who ruled her household with an iron fist. She habitually wore black-lace dresses, lace caps, and a cape with a stand-up, beaded collar. Local residents laughed behind her back and took to calling her "Queen Victoria" in private.

Christopher Crawley died at Monte Cristo on December 14, 1910, at age sixty-nine. The constant rubbing of his starched collars resulted in a gangrenous abscess on his neck, which, in turn, caused his heart to fail. Following his death, Elizabeth retreated into deep mourning, converting an upstairs box room into a chapel that she rarely left. In fact, she is reputed to have left the homestead only twice in the twenty-three years between her husband's death

and her own death, from a ruptured appendix, on August 12, 1933, at age ninety-two.

In 1948, the last of the Crawleys left the homestead, and Monte Cristo fell victim to rot and vandalism.

Years later in 1955, Reginald Ryan, a tailor from Wagga Wagga, drove past Monte Cristo and felt an instant but eerie connection. He somehow knew he was destined to live there. Sure enough, eight years later on June 3, 1963, Reginald, his wife, Olive, and their three children moved into their new home, which Reginald then set about restoring to its former glory. The family still live alongside their spiritual lodgers, and an uneasy truce prevails. For any outside visitors, however, it is quite a different story.

By far the strongest ghostly presence in the homestead is that of Elizabeth Crawley. She is most often seen in the converted chapel, wearing black and carrying a large silver cross. Her presence is extremely domineering, and she is very particular about what goes on in her house and does her best to unsettle any guests. She has been known to order people out of the dining room, and an icy atmosphere descends whenever her spirit is present.

The sound of loud footsteps on hard wooden floors can be heard around the house. This is unsettling, but even more so when you consider that the whole house is now carpeted.

An apparition of a young woman in period dress has been seen gliding slowly along the front balcony. A pregnant maid jumped to her death from this very spot. The blood-stained steps below were cleaned with bleach, but to this day, you can still see the discoloration.

The second story of the house has witnessed at least three deaths. A young woman died after a particularly long and tortuous labor, and Christopher Crawley himself died in what is now known as the boys' bedroom. Sad faces are often seen staring in through the second-story windows even though there is no balcony outside.

The atmosphere surrounding the staircase is one of the most disturbing in the whole house. Today, many young children become extremely frightened and agitated when in the vicinity. Some have even been known to have asthma attacks. This is less surprising when you learn that the Crawley's baby girl was dropped from her nanny's arms down the stairs to her death. The horrified nanny claimed that the baby had been pushed out of her arms by an unseen force. Whatever the truth of the matter, a menacing aura still lingers.

Outside the house, the forlorn figure of a vulnerable young boy is often seen loitering in the vicinity of the coach house. This was the scene of the tragic death of a stable lad named Morris, who slept in the stables but was too ill to get up for work one day. His boss did not believe him and set fire to his bedding. Poor Morris was too sick to escape and burned to death where he lay.

The most recent tragedy happened in 1961, after a local youth had watched repeated showings of the movie *Psycho*. Late at night he crept up to the grounds of the homestead carrying his rifle and shot dead the caretaker, Jackie Simpson. To this day you can see the words "Die Jack Ha Ha" inscribed in a macabre scrawl on the wooden door of the caretaker's cottage.

Monte Cristo has been featured on many television programs and has been visited by many paranormal investigators. No one has ever come away without seeing something strange or feeling very uncomfortable. This melancholy old mansion house is open to the public, so go visit, if you dare.

The Street with No Name

Boys and girls come out to play,
The moon doth shine as bright as day.
Leave your supper and leave your sleep
And join your play fellows in the street.

There is a narrow, overgrown pathway running alongside a railway viaduct in Annandale, Sydney. It is known locally as "The Street with No Name." It is a desolate place, dark and deeply foreboding, especially at night. It even has its own colony of bats. Along with the surrounding park area, The Street with No Name has borne witness to a host of heinous crimes.

Its deeply disturbing history can be traced back to 1968, when the mutilated body of a three-year-old boy was found half hidden in the damp undergrowth. This abominable murder has never been solved. A mere eight years later, the body of a twelve-year-old boy was found nearby, with hideous and extensive head injuries, inflicted, apparently, by a large rock. Unbelievably, seven months later in almost the exact same spot, the body of another twelve-year-old boy was found. This wretched child had died from multiple stab wounds to the chest, stomach, and legs. In 1977 a man was arrested and charged with the murders of the two twelve-year-olds.

A year earlier however, in 1976, the body of a young girl was found unceremoniously dumped in the nearby car park. Details of this killing are not forthcoming, but it is rumored to be one of Sydney's first satanic murders.

Not surprisingly, with its terrifyingly gory history, this place is now awash with sinister sightings and eerie feelings. Young children and dogs behave in a bizarre manner when anywhere within the vicinity. In fact, only the boldest or stupidest of children would dare to venture near after being brought up with warnings to stay well away.

One unfortunate victim, a homeless man named Reg Malvin, had been repeatedly warned not to sleep in the surrounding park area. He ignored the warnings and in early 2000 was found bludgeoned to death. A section of timber floorboards from the bandstand on which he was found had to be replaced to remove evidence of the gruesome bloodstains left there.

There is a warren of unused storage rooms beneath the viaduct. One of these storage rooms is leased out to a Mark Brynes, who uses it as a photographic studio. It has been nicknamed the "Tomb." The body of the first murdered twelve-year-old was found right outside the Tomb's window. Mark has often heard ghostly footsteps coming from this area.

Visitors to the Tomb have reported a variety of unsettling sightings and sensations. There is always an overwhelming feeling of being watched, the classic hair-raising experience. One unfortunate visitor reported feeling stabbing sensations below his ribs and in his lower back. Feelings of nausea and sudden headaches are very common. There have been reports of strange and unpleasant odors, bright lights, and unexplained cold breezes in an otherwise draft-free room.

Outside of the Tomb the gloomy pathway is particularly unnerving with the sounds of phantom footsteps and the rustling of leaves vibrating in the still air. Strange orbs of light have been seen and photographed floating along the cursed pathway. Many wonder whether these are the souls of two of the murdered children.

On December 12, 2001, a group of paranormal investigators visited The Street with No Name. One member of the team reported feeling very anxious and panicky behind the viaduct, as though something was about to happen. She felt most disturbed in a small clearing in the middle, commenting that it was a very unpleasant place to be. Another member, upon entering the Tomb, immediately noticed a strange odor, which others commented on, too. He felt a pressure on his chest that made it difficult for him to breathe and experienced waves of nausea. Outside on the pathway, the investigators experienced a very strong sensation that they were disturbing someone, although it was obvious no one was there. They heard footsteps walking on the empty ground ahead, and all agreed that the feelings they felt were some of the most appalling they had ever experienced.

One final apparition, often seen in the area and maybe not quite as menacing, is that of a tenderhearted railway worker named Jock. He had apparently walked along the railway tracks to rescue an injured possum when a train thundered out of the thick fog and plowed straight into him. Locals swear that on foggy nights they can still see him floating above the tracks, and hear the sounds of him searching for other animals in need of help.

The Street with No Name is awash with sorrow; the horrors it has witnessed have left an indelible mark. Pity the poor souls imprisoned in its murky shadows.

The Mayanup Poltergeist

Australian Aboriginal tribes have as many different customs and beliefs as they have languages. Binding them all is a common belief in the importance of the land and their role in respecting and protecting it. Specific areas of land are much hallowed; threats from modern development, construction, and farming can cause the Aborigines much distress. Language presents no barrier for the different tribes; they talk of a spiritual connection called "Songlines," like an underground stream, bringing spiritual dreams that communicate any impending threats to the land or to hallowed ground.

All language groups place great emphasis on the land in their death rituals, believing that the spirits of the dead pass on to Dreaming Ancestors in the land, so long as the correct ceremonial rituals are performed. Mourning is accompanied by special dances and by a low wailing, a type of mournful "song," that eases the passage of the spirit into Dreamworld. Many Aborigines believe that a person has two spirits: one is harmless; the other is anything but. Without the correct burial, the harmful spirit, unable to join its Dreaming Ancestors, will haunt the living and cause mischief.

On the night of May 17, 1955, Gilbert and Jean Smith, an Aboriginal couple employed as farm workers on Keninup Farm in Boyup Brook, were settling down for the night in their simple camp, when the peace was shattered by a bizarre phenomenon that was to plague the family for another three years.

The Smiths' home was being bombarded by a shower of rocks, materializing from nowhere and bouncing off the thin roof of the building. A disembodied, low, mournful, wailing noise, reminiscent of an Aboriginal death song, sent shivers through the Smiths and drove their dogs berserk. The animals instantly broke free from their tethers and disappeared into the night, mad with terror. Whatever spirit was responsible for these events was making it clear from the start that it was far from happy.

The activities quickly escalated. The spirit, which became known as "the Jannick," demonstrated its considerable power, seemingly creating stones and hurling them at the Smiths and their home from the inside as well as the outside. Rocks would suddenly appear swirling around inside the family's hurricane lamps, or trapped like popcorn under bedding. They would rain down from the ceiling and batter the kitchen table. The rocks were always warm, and often accompanied by strange orbs of colored light, either orange or blue, that would move either randomly or at other times with intelligent direction, sinisterly following a member of the family around. Most menacing were the times when incandescent spectral hands would be seen in the act of throwing.

The poltergeist activity soon began to attract the attention of the press, and a somewhat skeptical Hugh Schmitt from the *Australian Post* was dispatched to keep vigil for a night at the Smiths' camp. His response in the *Post* following his terrifying ordeal that night was simple: "This thing is no hoax!" His experiences began before he had even gotten out of his car, when stones were hurled out of thin air. He, like many others who kept vigil at the house over the course of the three years, swore that the activity in the house defied the laws of physics and could therefore not be accounted for by any human activity.

When close friends of the Smiths, employed as farm workers on a neighboring farm, visited to offer their support, they were horrified to discover that the entity had followed them back to their own camp. Then, in 1957, over 180 miles away in a town called Pumphrey, identical activity was reported, again targeting the Aboriginal employees of another farmer, Alan Donaldson. Both of these incidents petered out, but for a while identical phenomena were occurring simultaneously in three places, despite the distance which separated them. The nature of the incidents and the fact that they all focused on Aboriginal farm workers gave rise to speculation that whatever was responsible for terrorizing the Smiths was also terrorizing the other two families. The Jannick became known by the name of the shire of Western Australia in which all incidents took place—Mayanup.

No one at the time, or since, has been able to offer a rational explanation for the Mayanup poltergeist. The rocks were methodically examined by scientists, who discovered they were simply ordinary local stone. Following any haunting, Aborigines hold an "inquest," at which an elder attempts to determine who has so wronged and angered the spirit, but whatever enraged the Jannick is still unexplained. When Gilbert Smith died, his wife Jean moved back into the city, but the poltergeist went with her. The Jannick has not shown itself since Jean Smith died, three years after the phenomenon began.

Recently, Helen Hack, the wife of the farm owner's son, who was six at the time of the events at his father's farm, researched the events that took place there in the fifties and has written a book about what she uncovered. She found the Smiths had not been the first people to have experienced the strange bobbing orbs of blue or orange light in the area, nor were they the last. The same lights had been described at the murder scene of an English boy, killed in 1900, and again in the 1970s, although by then they had been interpreted locally as UFO sightings. If these orb-sightings are one and the same, perhaps we have not heard the last from the Mayanup poltergeist.

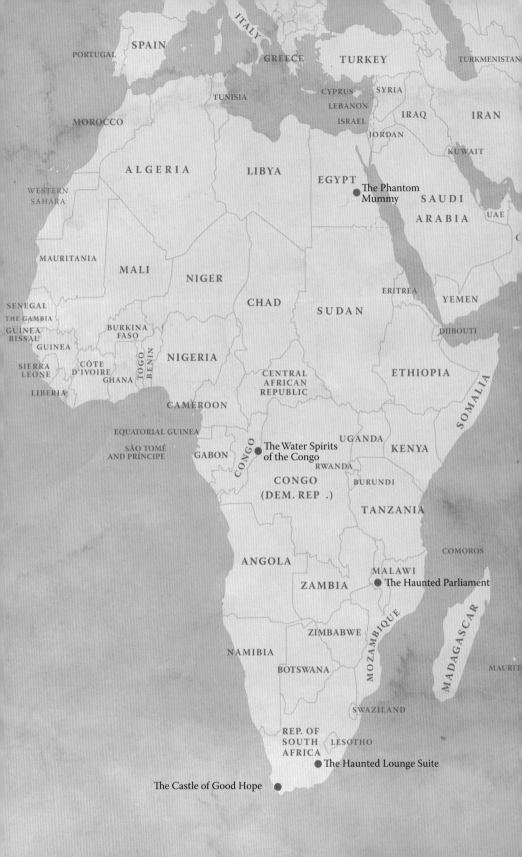

PORTUGAL
SPAIN
ITALY
GREECE
TURKEY
TURKMENISTAN

TUNISIA
CYPRUS
SYRIA
LEBANON
ISRAEL
IRAQ
IRAN

MOROCCO
JORDAN
KUWAIT

WESTERN
SAHARA
ALGERIA
LIBYA
EGYPT
● The Phantom
Mummy
SAUDI
ARABIA
UAE

MAURITANIA
MALI
NIGER
CHAD
SUDAN
ERITREA
YEMEN
DJIBOUTI

SENEGAL
THE GAMBIA
GUINEA
BISSAU
GUINEA
BURKINA
FASO
NIGERIA
ETHIOPIA
SOMALIA

SIERRA
LEONE
CÔTE
D'IVOIRE
GHANA
TOGO
BENIN
CENTRAL
AFRICAN
REPUBLIC

LIBERIA
CAMEROON

EQUATORIAL GUINEA
SÃO TOMÉ
AND PRÍNCIPE
GABON
CONGO
● The Water Spirits
of the Congo
UGANDA
KENYA
RWANDA

CONGO
(DEM. REP.)
BURUNDI
TANZANIA

COMOROS

ANGOLA
MALAWI
● The Haunted Parliament
ZAMBIA

MADAGASCAR

ZIMBABWE
MOZAMBIQUE
MAURIT

NAMIBIA
BOTSWANA

SWAZILAND

REP. OF
SOUTH
AFRICA
LESOTHO
● The Haunted Lounge Suite

The Castle of Good Hope ●

Africa

The spiritual beliefs of the peoples of Africa weave into the heart of their oral traditions a respect for the spirits of their dead. For some of Africa's visitors, the breathtaking beauty of the continent captured their hearts and souls so completely, even death couldn't tear them away.

The Castle of Good Hope

CAPE TOWN, SOUTH AFRICA

Don't be reassured by the name of this seventeenth-century fortress, which faces the sea in Cape Town. The history of the Castle of Good Hope is bleak, bloody, and tortuous. For centuries, its dungeons have echoed with the agonized death cries of escaped slaves, convicts, outlaws, and even the Zulu King Cetewayo and his wives who were incarcerated there. The worst of all these cells is a windowless hellhole known as *Die Donker Gat* (The Dark Hole), which would reportedly flood in minutes during the winter flood seasons, drowning any prisoners instantly as they stood helplessly chained to the walls.

Further miseries have etched themselves into the psychic spectrum that lies within the walls of this pentagonal castle, not least of which were two suicides, one notoriously involving a soldier stationed in the castle who was found hanging from the castle's bell-rope. Strange, unpredictable tolling of this bell, along with periodic sightings of a shimmering, luminescent figure—nearing seven feet in height and pacing the battlements linking two of the castle's bastions—has given rise to speculation that the spirit of this poor unfortunate, who ended his days in the bell tower, has never been able to fully break free from the scene of his death. The figure has even been seen leaping over the battlements, thereby avoiding imminent contact with approaching humans. Footsteps are heard frequently along empty sections of the same stretch.

Arguably the most chilling incident of all involved a man named Pieter Gysbert van Noodt, one of the Cape's eighteenth-century colonial governors. Van Noodt was a notoriously harsh man who had little sympathy for any

soldier found slacking or deserting. In 1729, the council at the Cape condemned seven soldiers to beating and deportation for attempted desertion.
Van Noodt was furious at what he perceived to be the leniency of the sentence
and overturned it, insisting the men be hanged. He steadfastly ignored all
pleas for leniency, and so came the morning when the soldiers were taken to
the gallows. As the last man was lead forward, he called aloud to God, asking
for divine justice to be visited upon Governor van Noodt. Immediately after
the hangings, van Noodt was found dead in his chair, his face terror-stricken,
apparently having suffered a heart attack.

Further intrigue adds to the tension of this story. A primary source discussing
Noodt's death, written by Captain Rudolph Allemann, alleges that the council
was so reluctant to give van Noodt a burial on sacred ground that his "official"
funeral was a fake, and that the rather grand coffin interred on the day was, in
fact, empty. Allemann insisted that van Noodt's body was buried elsewhere in
a cheap coffin and in an unmarked grave. A man as fierce in life as van Noodt
would surely have been sorely incensed by such an ignoble funeral.

It would seem that such was his wrath that he has never left the castle since.
To this day, those who work in and visit the castle attribute strange occurrences to van Noodt's ghost. Lights turning on and off inexplicably, sounds of
arguments, and the setting off of electric bells in the guard's room are commonly reported. Recently, a group of tourists visiting the castle's dungeons
suddenly discovered themselves trapped inside for over an hour. No matter
how much they cried for help and banged on the doors and walls, their pleas
remained unanswered. Finally, with fears mounting as air grew thin, they
found the strength to break down the dungeon door and were free. The tour
leaders remain convinced that this bears the van Noodt hallmark.

The castle holds other terrors: the ghost of a large black hound that leaps
angrily at visitors only to disappear in the moment before impact; a portrait
of another unpopular governor that has such a powerful aura, dogs won't

pass it without growling and snarling; and a portrait of peacocks, to which is attached a legend that it threatens anyone who moves it with certain death. (It has been speculated that the portrait hides a safe full of long forgotten treasure belonging to the Dutch East India Company that originally built the castle, or a secret passageway connecting the castle with Government House.)

Over the years, a mysterious lady in gray has been seen by many witnesses including, allegedly, the late Princess Margaret of the British Royal Family during the 1947 royal tour. The serene figure has also been seen at Government House, now called Tuynhuys, adding to the mystery of a secret passageway that is said to connect it to the castle.

There is one final specter that has been sighted around the castle that helps to counterbalance the site's more sinister and foreboding presences. She is a lady whose residence brought art and music to the castle. She wrote and painted extensively about the castle and the Cape; she created a ballroom, threw lavish parties, and bathed in the secluded dolphin pool within the castle grounds. Lady Anne Barnard loved the castle that became her home in the late eighteenth century.

Her ballroom was still in use right up until the South African Army left the castle in the late twentieth century. There are several reports of her translucent, curly-haired ghost joining parties thrown for important guests throughout that period. Others hope that the dolphin pool, recently renovated according to Lady Ann's descriptions and illustrations, will be the site for further sightings of the lady who once loved to bathe there nude, in the eighteenth-century fashion.

The Haunted Lounge Suite

In South Africa, the phenomenon of poltergeist haunting is known by the indigenous term of *tokoloshe*. *Tokoloshe* hauntings often involve spirits that are merely mischievous; when incidents turn more sinister, locals believe that the spirit has fallen under the influence of a witch. Local shamans (known as *inyanga* or *sangoma*) can exorcise *tokoloshe* spirits with the aid of a carefully manufactured powder, widely sold by shamans all over the region. *Tokoloshe* incidents in South Africa and in Zimbabwe are taken very seriously and are widely feared.

In September 1998, the South African press reported a unique case of a *tokoloshe* haunting. Ms. Nothemba Bekebhu was a forty-two-year-old woman from Queenstown, and a highly respected member of her community. She worked as a special educational needs specialist and as a *sangoma*.

She returned home from work one evening to be confronted with the strange sight of five *tokoloshe* spirits sitting on her couches. They all had a vaguely human appearance, although they were disturbingly devoid of facial features. Her terror turned to startled confusion when the *tokoloshe* spoke to her and issued a peculiar demand: *equal housing rights with living souls*. They insisted that Ms. Bekebhu contact President Mandela's office to pursue their claim. She duly called the president's office, and was told that they could only take action if they were able to speak directly with a *tokoloshe* spokesperson. Bekebhu was not able to persuade any *tokoloshe* to come to the phone.

The *tokoloshe* continued to torment the woman and took possession of her lounge suite to the extent that she was driven to distraction. In October 1998, the Eastern Cape newspaper, the *Daily Dispatch*, carried a story describing how a reporter named Mkhululi Titi had arrived at the house to interview Ms. Bekebhu and had found her in a state of some considerable distress. Her lounge was thick with the smoke from burning plates of her *sangoma* medicines, called *mutis*, that she hoped would drive the spirits away.

She explained that she had reached a breaking point as a result of the poltergeist activity in her home. She had turned to her local police for help, and had the receiver in her hand as she opened the door to the reporter. The article describes how, "She was pushing the handset of the phone under the couch so that police could hear the *tokoloshe*s talking." A spokesperson from the local police told the *Daily Dispatch* that they were at a loss as to how they could help Ms. Bekebhu as "she was not being intimidated by human beings."

With no one else to turn to for help, Ms. Bekebhu was forced to take the dramatic step of vacating her home.

The Haunted Parliament

N ew State House, just outside Lilongwe, Malawi's capital, is a vast, opulent palace, consisting of more than three hundred rooms that took a staggering twenty years and a hundred million dollars to build. It is the Presidential residence, as well as the traditional housing for the country's parliament, and stands in beautiful grounds which extend for more than thirteen hundred acres. Extravagance on this scale amid a nation struggling with poverty has been the cause of much contention in the country. It is also the unlikely setting for one of Malawi's most controversial ghost stories.

President Bingu wa Mutharika attracted much international attention early in 2005 when he moved out of his mansion residence, evicting Parliament from the building and forcing the government to consider renting a sports stadium and several motels so it could continue with its business. A senior government aide told journalists that the reason for such a rash and costly decision was that President Mutharika was plagued by ghosts. Astonished members of the press were told how the President was tormented by ghost rodents each night as he lay trying to sleep. He would feel them crawling all over his body, but as he turned on the lights, they would vanish. Another aide, insisting on anonymity before agreeing to disclose any information, explained that the President was tormented by the sounds of footsteps and strange, unearthly noises in his Presidential suite at night.

He is alleged to have called upon the services of clergy to exorcise evil spirits in the palace. The country's Presidential aide on Christian affairs, the Reverend Malani Mtonga, initially said, "It's true that the president is no longer

staying there and we have asked clerics from several Christian churches including the Roman Catholic to pray for the new state house to exorcise evil spirits. . . . No strategy designed from the pits of hell will prosper against the president because we have asked for divine intervention to cast the blood of Jesus against any evil plots against the president."

Interestingly, two previous Malawian Presidents are also famed for refusing to remain in the presidential palace at Lilongwe. And the country has a history of presidents who claim to have been tormented by the spirits of the dead. Malawi's first two presidents, Hastings Kamuzu Banda and Baliki Muluzi, who occupied the Sanjika Palace in the town of Blantyre, were also troubled by ghostly visitors. President Banda was plagued by the spirits of two mysterious dwarfs. President Muluzi was purported to have been tormented by the spirit of a prominent Malawian politician who had been killed in a road accident under mysterious circumstances. Muluzi claimed to have come face to face with the ghost in the long, dark, deserted corridors of the palace late at night after a hard day's work. The President was prepared to stick it out, refusing to let any soul, living or otherwise, deny him his right to reside at the Palace. But the breaking point came when his wife and several of their children began suffering permanent headaches and were repeatedly awoken in the night, terrified and shivering, hearing a series of eerie, unnatural noises. The First Family retreated from the Palace.

Their unearthly troubles were widely discussed and accepted by Malawians at the time: Malawi people recognize that they share their country with a very real spectral presence. Robert Jamieson, the editor of the Malawian newspaper, *The Chronicle*, said that Malawians "accept the issue of ghosts and spirits as a reality. We talk about it all the time." Another journalist, Sharon LaFraniere of the *New York Times*, also acknowledged the central role the belief in ghosts has in modern Malawi. "It was not unthinkable that a former World Bank economist like Mutharika, highly skilled in such matters as how to conquer inflation and spur development, might fret about the possibility of spirits. In many parts of sub-Saharan Africa, traditional superstitions coexist seamlessly with modern sensibilities."

Yet these views do not appear to be shared by the current President of Malawi. Strangely, when the story was first published, a furor broke out in the Presidential quarters. The Reverend Mtonga instantly changed his story, denying that he had ever spoken to reporters on the subject. The President himself insisted, "I have never feared ghosts in my life." He then took the extreme step of having two reporters arrested, on the grounds that under an ancient colonial-era statute, it was illegal to ridicule the President. Raphael Tenthani, a BBC reporter, and Mabvuto Banda, who writes for Reuters, were arrested on March 15, 2005.

As the Director of Public Prosecutions Ishmael Wadi released the two men, he told Malawi state television that the men had been charged with "causing ridicule to the high office of the president." Despite the many other pressing issues that must face those responsible for the running of a country, the Malawian government took a further surprising decision: the entire Media and Communications Parliamentary Committee met with the two journalists to discuss the case and explain parliament's position. Whatever the truth about the ghost rodents of the Presidential suite, there could be little doubt that parliament was treating the matter very seriously indeed. Maybe, as some presidential aides quietly speculated, it was the implication that the experience had caused the Head of State to lose his cool and flee in terror that had most angered President Mutharika.

Curiously, despite the public relations disaster that had been caused by moving out of New State House, President Mutharika chose not to return immediately; instead he remained in a palace in Kasungu, making a sixty-mile journey into the capital every day.

The Water Spirits of the Congo

The people of the Congo and other parts of Central and Western Africa embrace the spirits of their dead ancestors and the influence they have over daily life, in a way that many Western cultures have shied away from over the centuries. Central to the spirituality of the Congo is the worship of the spirits of these ancestors, who are regularly invoked in their religious ceremonies; there are no "hauntings" in the traditional sense of the word. Spirits are seen as a concrete entities; calling the spirit to show itself can be achieved in a variety of ways, most commonly by entering into a trance-like state, often through dance.

In the Congo there is a hierarchy of spirits. The recently dead, those relatives who are nameable, are known as *nkuyu*. One step above them are spirits known as the *simbi* (the plural is *bisimbi*). Once a *simbi* is in the presence of the living it is fed. Some *simbi* express a preference for spirits of an alcoholic nature, in particular whiskey. The spirits offer advice and wisdom to the congregation and in some cases carry out healings.

These spirits are further removed from humans and the locality in which they lived their life. They have often been given a region over which they are asked to offer protection. *Bisimbi* haunt fresh water sources, usually rivers, and have an unpredictable nature; they certainly are much feared and their benevolence is never taken for granted. Kavuna Simon, a Congo man, wrote about the terrifying force of the *simbi* spirits in the early twentieth century:

Truly they have great power and authority, for their power is
revealed by the force they show in the water and in the gullies.
They stir up very high winds and unleash tornadoes, so that the
bodies of people are filled with fear and trembling. They break
people's courage and render it feeble, weak, limp, petrified, hollow
and fevered; they are stunned and grovel in terror. This is how
the bisimbi *show their strength: if they see someone come to draw*
water from the pool where they reside, they rise to the surface and
cover it with foam and turbulence, turning and twisting. So the
person drawing the water is scared stiff when she sees how the water
boils in the pool. She may tumble into the water because she is
dizzy. If she does not cry out so that those who remain in the village
hear her, when next they meet her she may be dead.

Bisimbi can affect a person's psyche, causing a change in personality or inducing a state of terror so strong that the person is left incapable—literally petrified. The water *simbi* of the Congo appear in vaguely human form, and, when angry are said to stir up the water to such an extent that women and children have been made disoriented and have drowned, sucked into the ferocious depths. Not surprisingly, *bisimbi* can also be associated with war and warriors.

Encounters with *bisimbi* can also have other physical manifestations. They are often associated with methods of fast communication. Nerve impulses, the Internet, and electricity—anything that moves at the speed of light—are potentially subject to *simbi* influence.

Connection with a *simbi* is believed to bring with it the possibility of the gifts of power, wealth, and insight, and is therefore actively sought by some, as much as it is feared by others. A traditional Congo story of a man who encountered a water *simbi* tells of a face-to-face manifestation of the spirit in a pond behind his house. The female *simbi* was of mesmerizing beauty, and day after day, the man returned to the pond, lured by her beauty. As the days went on, the man and his family began to experience a marked change in their fortunes and were convinced that the *simbi* was responsible for endowing them with their new wealth. The man continued his daily quest to rendezvous with the *simbi*, heedless of the potential danger of entering into such a perilous bargain.

Finally, one day, as his family lay anxiously awaiting his return, the *simbi's* goodwill ended, and, enraged by his greed, she stirred up the waters in the pond, sucking the man beneath the water and dragging him down to his watery grave. His body was never found.

The Phantom Mummy

The ancient land of Egypt is awash with mystery, from the deadly secrets of its unique pyramids to our fascination with its once advanced civilization. Its glorious history of colorful Pharaohs and indecipherable hieroglyphics exerts an extraordinary power over us to this day. Among the crumbling ruins and looted tombs of a land of mystical speculation there remain tales of curses and hauntings of horror beyond belief.

The Princess Amen-Ra lived in Egypt some 1,500 years B.C. Upon her death she was mummified, laid in an exquisitely decorated sarcophagus, and buried deep in the bowels of a pyramid upon the banks of the Nile in Luxor.

During the 1890s, a group of Englishmen with money in their pockets visited the excavations at Luxor and were fascinated to witness the unearthing of a perfectly preserved coffin which was identified as that of the Princess Amen-Ra. In those days artifacts were sold to the highest bidder with no thought given to the preservation of history. After much bartering, one of the men bought the coffin and had it sent to his hotel room. Not long afterwards he was seen walking purposefully towards the desert where he disappeared forever into the vast sands. In the following days and months, each of the remaining three men encountered various misfortunes. One of the men was accidentally shot in the arm and later had to have it amputated. The second man fell seriously ill and as a consequence lost his job, while the third man returned to England to find himself destitute, his entire savings lost on the stock market.

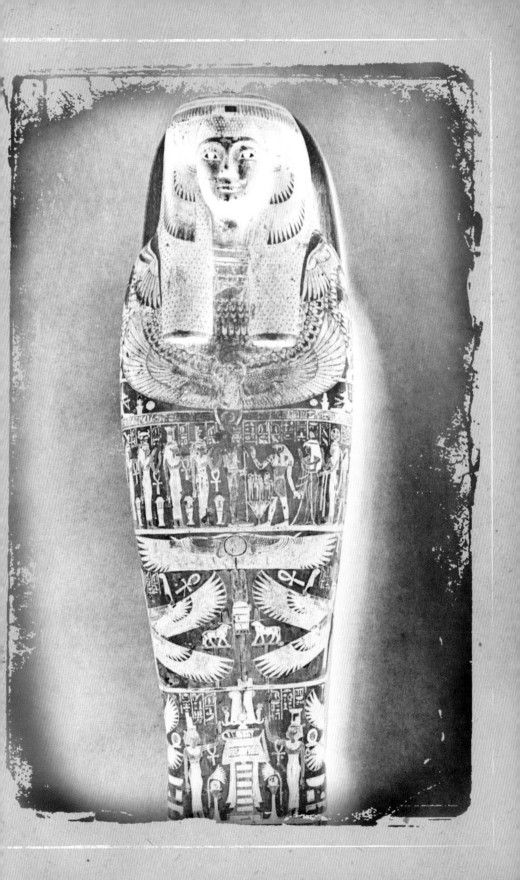

How the coffin ended up in England is a mystery, but it was eventually bought some years later by a rich London businessman to add to his collection of rare Egyptian artifacts. The unfortunate man and his family were to experience a catalogue of horrendous disasters including the accidental death of three family members and the burning down of their house. Fearing the Egyptian coffin had something to do with the suffering which had so abruptly entered his life, the businessman donated the coffin to the British Museum.

The misery continued even as the coffin was being transported. One of the two workmen employed to carry the coffin to the museum fell and broke his leg; the other workman died suddenly a few days later.

The coffin was placed in the Egyptian Room at the museum and it was here that the enraged spirit of Princess Amen-Ra truly made her presence felt. The museum's night watchmen began to hear disturbing noises coming from inside the coffin. Loud knocking and frenzied scratching sounds echoed through the room. They often heard cries of frustration and the mournful reverberation of deep and prolonged sobbing. Upon entering the Egyptian Room in the morning they would find that other exhibits had been tossed and hurled around the room. The watchmen grew more fearful and reluctant to turn up for their shifts. When one night watchman died while on duty, the others resigned in terror. The museum's cleaners also refused to go anywhere near the coffin after hearing of a visitor who flicked the dust from the face of the coffin with his handkerchief, only to have his son die from measles the very next day.

The museum authorities decided enough was enough and had the haunted sarcophagus moved to the basement. Once again one of the removal men fell seriously ill, and the supervisor in charge of the move was found dead at his desk.

Of course by now Princess Amen-Ra had gained mass notoriety and stories surrounding her evil spirit began to be printed in the papers. A young news reporter traveled to the museum to take a photograph of the feared coffin. Upon developing the photograph he was stunned to see the most horrifying image of a face staring out at him. The shaken fellow took himself home and shot himself. We can only wonder what he saw in the eyes of that face.

Eventually, the British Museum found a private collector willing to buy the now famously possessed coffin. The buyer immediately began to experience a host of adverse phenomena and called upon the services of Madame Helena Blavatsky, a well-known psychic expert. On entering the house she at once began to shiver and sweat. She refused to exorcise the coffin and implored the owner to rid himself of the evil as soon as possible.

This proved a difficult task, as by now no museum would touch the cursed coffin and anyone with a concern for their own safety knew to steer well clear. Perhaps it is little surprise, then, that today the exact location of the sarcophagus is a hotly debated mystery. All that can be said for sure is that the spirit of Princess Amen-Ra will not be pacified until she has been duly laid to rest once more in Luxor.

RUSSIAN

FEDERATION

KAZAKHSTAN

MONGOLIA

NORTH
KOREA

SOUTH
KOREA

CHINA

The Haunted Well of
Himeji Castle

JA

The Ghost Climbers of
the Himalayas

NEPAL

BHUTAN

The Haunted
Campus

The Hungry
Ghosts

BANGLADESH

TAIWAN

INDIA

BURMA

LAOS

THAILAND

VIETNAM

PHILIPPIN

Nang Naak's Shrine

CAMBODIA

MALAYSIA

The Haunted Beaches
of Singapore

INDONESI

Asia

Asia is a continent of contrasts. Encounters with spirits are just as varied, ranging from war sites to ancient burial grounds to the great Mount Everest. From the metropolitan cities of the Orient to the soaring heights of the Himalayas, the common reverence its people share for their dead remains a constant.

The Ghost Climbers of the Himalayas

The Himalayas, in all their breathtaking beauty, have a spiritual significance for the people that live in their shadow. Mount Everest, the world's highest mountain, is one of five peaks in the Himalayas that are home to a group of goddesses known as the Five Sisters of Long Life, of which the most revered is believed to reside on Mount Chomolhari. The sanctity of this mountain is still respected today, both by locals and by visitors from around the globe, and it is off-limits to climbers.

But every year, climbers challenge their limits of endurance by making the ascent to, and (what is often the more dangerous) descent from, the summit of one of the other peaks of the Himalayan range, in particular Everest and Kangchenjunga. The climb takes enormous physical and psychological strength and resilience. Weather conditions and oxygen supplies present constantly changing challenges. Not all will survive; often, despite all the experience, training, and preparation, a bad fall or a sudden storm makes the difference between life and death.

But there is another factor that seems to influence the outcome of difficult climbs. Many of those who are familiar with Everest and Kangchenjunga have witnessed on their glistening snow-covered faces the miraculous impact of the phantom climbers. Others have reported witnessing from a distance the progress of a climber they know cannot be there. The ghost climbers of the Himalayas have encouraged people to the top, and have led people safely back to base camp. Medics explain these apparitions as a delusion caused by oxygen starvation at high-altitude—in many cases this may well be the

cause. But on Everest and Kangchenjunga, the ghost climbers are seen at all altitudes, often below the 28,000 feet at which hypoxia is believed to trigger hallucinations.

On June 20, 2003, an experienced Spanish climber, Carlos Pauner, and his Italian teammates successfully reached the summit of Kangchenjunga. They began the descent to Camp III at 25,000 feet in deteriorating weather conditions. Pauner lagged behind, keeping in touch with his team by torchlight signals. After a grueling descent over steep, rocky terrain and in ever worsening weather, his teammates made it to Camp III by 1 A.M., more than eight hours after reaching the summit. Pauner was nowhere to be seen. Throughout the rest of that night, the team kept watch, leaving lights shining into the night and shouting for Pauner. There was no reply. By 9 A.M. the following morning, the men had serious frostbite and were forced to begin the descent to base camp. There was still no sign of Pauner.

Pauner had still been at an altitude of 26,000 feet when night had fallen. In the storm and the dark, he suddenly became aware that he was no longer alone. He could not see his companion, but nevertheless heard a voice encouraging him to rest. Pauner refused; an experienced mountain climber knows the dangers of sleep in extreme weather conditions. But the voice continued to persuade him, telling him he had worked so hard he deserved a sleep. In the end, the two men agreed to compromise; Pauner would walk another hundred steps and then rest a while. Throughout the night, the ghost climber stayed with Pauner, arguing with him all the while.

Pauner never did find Camp III, but after two days on the mountain, he made it to Camp II. Finally, with dying battery power, his headlamp signals were spotted from base camp and two Sherpas went to meet him and help him make the journey safely back. He suffered severe frostbite and needed rehydration but was alive.

Pauner wasn't the first climber to describe a supportive presence. In 1975, Dougal Haston and Doug Scott revealed that they were accompanied on their ascent of Everest by a ghost climber, who even shared their tent with them. The companion warned Scott where the dangerous areas of the climb would be. Another climber, F. S. Smythe, believed his ghost climber was so tangible that he tried to offer him some Kendal Mint Cake.

In Andrew Greig's book, *Kingdoms of Experience*, his 1985 ascent on Everest is described. Two of his teammates, Mal Duff and Chris Watts, were camped in a snow cave on the northeastern ridge of Mount Everest, when they heard the unmistakable noise of a fellow climber outside and his footsteps around the cave. Neither man felt brave enough to go and investigate. Some time later back at base camp, the two men, along with Liz Duff and Greig himself, watched through their binoculars a ghost climber on a solo ascent. That day everyone on the mountain had been accounted for; all three of them knew there could be no other climber. They watched him for an hour until another teammate walked into camp and distracted them. When they turned back to the climber, he had vanished.

Greig said of the incident, "I felt like we'd been watching for an hour an event that happened three years ago and was still somehow imprinted on the Ridge itself." Three years earlier, in 1982, Pete Boardman and Joe Tasker had disappeared on the same ridge.

The Five Sisters of Long Life cannot guarantee long life to all those who brave their ascent, but it seems they try to do their best.

The Haunted Beaches of Singapore

SINGAPORE

The people of Singapore's capital have many ghost stories to tell. Belief in ghosts is an integral part of local culture, making some citizens of the city more open to paranormal experiences. There are stories of haunted buildings all over Singapore, but paranormal activity has recently developed a new and unexpected focus. Stories of ghostly encounters, disembodied humming and crying, strange presences or auras, and even mild poltergeist activity at the city's beaches are being reported with alarming regularity.

Changi Beach on the East Coast is an idyllic stretch of pure white soft sand, shaded by trees and lapped by the deep blue waters of the ocean. It is a perfect holiday destination or weekend hideaway for city workers—hardly the type of location where one would expect a disturbing paranormal experience.

A row of huts for rent line the shore. Many families who have stayed in them have had a far from restful time. Most have left with an unshakeable feeling of having been watched by unseen eyes for the duration of their stay. They are the lucky ones. In many huts, people have reported spending sleepless nights listening to the constant opening and closing of the door, despite all their efforts to secure it. A few unlucky visitors have been awoken with a start by the disembodied sound of a woman crying close by. Others report being slapped in the face by a spectral hand, both in the hut and while bathing. And in very rare cases, people have seen a fleeting image of a wraith-like woman.

Punggol Beach, further along the coastline, was the site of the execution of nearly four hundred Chinese residents in 1948. People living close to the

188

beach regularly hear cries for help and the sound of gunfire; sometimes the sound is so clear that one or two of them have run to help. Of course they usually find the same thing: an empty beach. On one chilling occasion, a woman witnessed the spectral image of a World War II execution taking place in front of her. As it disappeared, she found a fresh bloodstain in the place she had seen the body fall.

The fishermen and anglers who spend their lives beside the ocean in Singapore have their own theories about the disturbances at the beaches. They feel that a growing disrespect for the ocean and the shoreline are angering these spirits. The authorities have plans to develop Punggol Beach; one fisherman questioned the wisdom of the development, saying simply, "We sure got trouble."

Nang Naak's Shrine,

BANGKOK, THAILAND

There is a particular site in Bangkok where the throngs of people and the thick sweet scent of incense assault your senses and give you the first indication that you are approaching a highly venerated site. In the grounds surrounding the shrine every tree has been tied with brightly colored ribbon, an offering to the spirits the Thai people believe reside in ancient trees. Inside, the shrine is piled high with gifts: flowers, food, and even women's dresses and cosmetics. In another section, children's clothing and toys are neatly stacked. The shrine is dedicated to Thailand's most feared and revered spirit, that of the young bride, Nang Naak.

There is much disagreement in Thailand about the factual details of the life of Nang Naak, also known by her original name, Mae Naak. Most believe that she was born in the second half of the nineteenth century, in either Bangkok or Ayutthaya. When she was a beautiful teenager, she met and fell in love with a handsome young man named Nai Maak. His family was poorer and of a lower social status than hers, and her father was incensed when the young couple announced their love for each other, but eventually he agreed to give his consent.

Their happiness was not to last long. Early in their married life, Nai Maak was conscripted to join the Thai army in the war against Cambodia. Desperately unhappy about his fate, Nai Maak had no choice but to go, leaving his young wife and their unborn child behind in Bangkok.

Nang Naak was never to have her longed-for reunion with her husband—at least not during her lifetime. After a long, agonizing labor, Nang Naak and her baby died, leaving her family devastated. Nai Maak, still fighting for his country in Cambodia, had no knowledge of what he would have to face upon his return home.

In Thai culture, the spirits of the deceased whose lives have been cut short may return to haunt the living if the body is cremated. Therefore, in keeping with these beliefs, Nang Naak's body was buried very quickly after her death. But so strong was her devotion to her husband that her spirit refused to lie still in the grave. When Nai Maak returned home from Cambodia, he saw exactly what he had longed for: his wife and child sitting at home, awaiting his return.

His family knew that the spirit of Nang Naak was not allowing her husband to see the new turn his life had taken during his absence. They vainly struggled to make him aware of the horrible truth. Then one day the grim reality was finally revealed to Nai Maak in a most macabre way. The couple's house was a traditional Thai stilted house; Nang Naak dropped a lime which fell through the slatted floorboards to the space beneath. Nai Maak watched in horror as Nang Naak reached for the lime, her hands slipping straight through the solid wood of the floorboards as if through water.

Nai Maak was finally able to see what his family had known all along. He fled from the specters of his dead wife and child in terror. The spirit of Nang Naak was deeply hurt by her husband's horrified departure. The romance of their story now turned irrevocably into horror.

Nang Naak pursued Nai Maak wherever he went, and the haunting became increasingly violent. He eventually remarried, but the venom of the spirit intensified and soon the entire village was terrorized by the ghost. Terrified and exhausted, Nai Maak and the villagers turned to a local Buddhist Temple for help. Nai Maak himself moved into the Temple, seeking refuge. The injuries the spirit inflicted continued to escalate, finally reaching a frenzied climax when the ghost killed a friend of Nai Maak's as he tried to intervene to offer some protection.

It took many monks to calm the tortured spirit of Nang Naak. When they finally succeeded, her body was reinterred, after the monks had first removed a piece of her skull.

But the story didn't end there. Sightings of Nang Naak's ghost continue all over Thailand to this day. In some stories she is described as a guardian angel, and young mothers recite a plea to Nang Naak to soothe their crying infants. She is also regarded by many young Thai as their protector against military conscription, which in Thailand is decided by lottery. Those wishing to avoid military conscription visit her shrine with gifts, hoping she will influence the lottery and prevent their call-up. And when the spirit of Nang Naak informed one medium that she would like to be allowed to watch television, two TV sets were instantly donated to her shrine, one of which remains on from morning till evening, every day.

In many other sightings, Nang Naak remains a menacing spirit. In recent years, the extreme fear that Nang Naak's ghost still commands in Thailand was brought under public scrutiny. The Thai press reported a story from Ayutthaya. A young couple in the city had committed suicide by hanging themselves. Their bodies were discovered together; the woman had been six months pregnant. In her suicide note, the woman had requested that both their bodies be cremated. Two local temples refused to carry out the dead woman's wishes, terrified of the paranormal repercussions if they did so. The parallels with Nang Naak were felt to be so strong that finally a surgeon was called upon to remove the body of the baby from its mother's womb before burial.

The Hungry Ghosts

During late summer, the Republic of China is a quiet and deserted place. A *frisson* of fear shimmers in the air and an aura of caution envelops the entire country. The beaches and recreation grounds have been abandoned, the roads and pavements are empty, weddings have been postponed, and important business deals rescheduled. Nobody dares to venture out after dark.

The reason for this widespread fear is the commencement of the seventh lunar month. It is the most dangerous time of the whole year. During this month the ghosts of the dead are released from hell to roam the earth once more, and the people of China take it very seriously.

Most of the ghosts are benign, content to visit their living relatives and bring about an uneasy reunion. But a small number of malicious ghosts spread terror. These are vengeful spirits which seek to harm the living; they have no descendants left on earth and often died a lonely death in tragic accidents or in desperate suicides. These souls are unfulfilled and wander in search of other souls, even those still living, to take their place in hell. They are the "hungry ghosts" and the Chinese do their utmost to pacify these malevolent spirits. They leave offerings of moon-cakes, sweet-smelling incense, and tempting bowls of traditional foods outside their houses. Paper lanterns are lit and set afloat on rivers to lead the evil spirits away from land.

The ghosts can take on many forms in order to wander the land unobserved. They are sometimes invisible and can be as light as a filmy cobweb. They can take the form of a bird, wolf, fox, or tiger padding softly through the darkness.

They adopt the form of a beautiful man or woman ready to seduce an unwary victim. They have been known to possess the body of an individual and cause illness and mental disorders. A particularly vigilant person will notice that the feet of a Chinese ghost never touch the ground.

The fifteenth day of the seventh month is the most perilous day of all. It is the day when the disturbed souls are at their strongest. People are advised to stay indoors, and if they must go out, to keep away from riverbanks where the malevolent spirits gather and where an unsuspecting passerby may have his soul snatched away.

On this day the temples are filled to overflowing with fruits, fish, vegetables, meat, and wines. Huge salvation poles are laid down to guide the spirits to the temples and away from where they are likely to do most harm.

On the last day of the seventh month the people of China heave a collective sigh of relief and pick up the threads of their normal lives. A Taoist priest recites a liturgy while holding a "Seven Star Sword" to let the restless spirits know it is time for them to return to the world beyond. The priest closes his ears to the pitiful wails of the wretched ghosts as they are sucked once more into the darkness.

However, not all the "hungry ghosts" are compliant and many remain in the land of the living ignoring all earthbound traditions. Throughout Chinese history there have been many strange incidents involving invisible and elusive spirits. Some of the most bizarre reports center on the activities of ponytail-removing poltergeists.

The Qing Dynasty was the last Imperial Dynasty in China (A.D. 1644-1911). The rulers of the Qing Dynasty at this time were the Manchu. They decreed that all men in China wear their hair braided into a pigtail, or queue, as a form of respect. A report dating from September 12, 1844, details an outbreak of pigtail cutting in the city of Taiyuan in the Shanxi Province. Respectable men would have their pigtails cut off in broad daylight while walking in busy streets, at the theater, or in bazaars. The perpetrators were said to vanish into thin air like specters. The phenomenon caused widespread panic and men fearing attack from behind held their pigtails in front. Soldiers were stationed in the streets and quack doctors sold charms to try and ward off attacks from the delinquent spirits.

Another outbreak occurred in 1876 in the Xiamen Province with many actual sightings of the "phantom barbers." The descriptions were many, but often involved tiny translucent phantoms seemingly made out of paper. One can only wonder what a Chinese ghost would want with a stolen pigtail.

The Chinese have a healthy attitude toward ghosts. They acknowledge their existence and strive to live in harmony, two worlds intermingling, with a modicum of respect.

The Haunted Campus

India is a deeply spiritual nation of over a billion people, an estimated seventy percent of whom are Hindus. Central to Hindu spirituality is the belief in reincarnation. In Hindu teaching, the soul is always alive, and when a person strives to lead a good life, the soul can attempt to break free from the cycle of death and rebirth, achieving eternal life or *moksha*. In Hindu belief, the soul of a person who dies a sudden or violent death steps out of this cycle of reincarnation to become a *bhut*, a ghost, temporarily confused and bewildered.

This is the story of just such a lost soul, unable to break free from the scene of his sudden and untimely death.

India is a scholarly nation boasting one of the highest number of university places of any nation on earth. Education is a commodity much valued by young Indian adults, so when the *Times of India* ran a story in September 2004 that the Indian Statistical Institute in Delhi had sent its students home for an unscheduled week's holiday, it caused some consternation.

In August 2004, a first-year student at the Institute collapsed and died in the middle of a class. His classmates were understandably distraught: a rare heart disorder caused his sudden death, although he had not previously shown any symptoms. But the shock of the tragedy was nothing compared to the harrowing ordeal that was to follow for the other students at the Institute.

The students became increasingly aware that the presence of their friend had not yet left the building. At first, there were intangible reminders: the scent of his aftershave clinging to the air or wafting down a corridor. Students would suddenly become aware of the scent as they turned a corner or entered a room. Then a female student, a non-smoker, became disturbed by a thick cloud of cigarette smoke that inexplicably filled her bathroom. Other students also remarked that cigarette smoke would suddenly overpower them in rooms where no one had been smoking. The boy who died had been a heavy smoker.

Strange noises were heard all over the student residences—footsteps pacing down empty corridors and disembodied knocking on doors. The students became increasingly uneasy. The scent and the sounds of the dead boy were becoming increasingly difficult to ignore.

The final phase of the haunting was to be the most disconcerting. Students climbing otherwise empty staircases began to lose their balance, feeling themselves suddenly jostled, as if someone had barged past them in a hurry. The experience was often accompanied by the familiar blast of the aftershave known to have been favored by the dead boy. It seems his *bhut* was becoming increasingly determined to announce its presence on campus.

The statisticians, renowned for their rational and scientific minds, became deeply uneasy about the paranormal entity lingering in their student residence. The Institute provided transportation for all who wished to travel to the local temple to meditate and pray for the repose of the spirit of their friend. However, when the students requested that a traditional Hindu prayer ritual take place on campus, the authorities were more reticent.

Many of the students who had directly experienced the spirit on campus felt that a *tantrik puja* was needed in order to release the spirit of their friend. A *tantrik puja* is a Hindu prayer to either a god or a spirit: in this case, the spirit of the dead student. In order to fully connect with the spirit, an object, painting, print, or sculpture becomes the focus of the *puja*, and Hindus believe the object becomes filled with the spirit's cosmic energy.

However, the authorities could not decide on the best course of action. Former students of the Institute discouraged them from indulging what their scientific minds dismissed as the "wild fears and mass hysteria" of the students. Finally, the unscheduled holiday was decided upon as a compromise.

Whatever the rationalists may have argued, only six of the statisticians at the Institute remained on campus. The others, their skeptical, scientific minds overwhelmed by the reality of their paranormal encounters, went home.

The Haunted Well of Himeji Castle

In Japanese culture, ghosts take on many different forms. *Yuurei* are ghosts whose deaths came about so suddenly that they did not have time to make their peace, either because they were murdered or committed suicide rashly (defeated warriors in Japan were often forced to commit suicide). Most hauntings by *yuurei* are of wronged female spirits; the theme common to all *yuurei* hauntings is revenge. This is the tale of a woman who was so deeply wronged in life that, after more than four hundred years, her soul remains hostage to the agony of the betrayal that killed her.

Himeji Castle is an imposing wooden construction, extremely well-preserved despite its age. It stands on an elevated position in the center of the town of Himeji, thirty miles west of Kobe. Known locally as the Heron Castle because of its protective covering of white plaster, it is dominated by a huge main tower soaring 150 feet above the skyline. The other characteristic feature of the castle is its complex labyrinthine defenses, where modern tourists still find themselves lost, despite clear signposts.

The castle's earliest origins are in the early fourteenth century, but it is in the seventeenth century, at a time when the local Shogun government commissioned the tower to be built to its five-story height, that this story is set. At the foot of the tower, known as the Donjon, and located next to the *Hara-kiri Maru* (the Suicide Gate), where people were forced to commit ritual disembowelment, stands the castle well. Its proximity to the gate is no mere coincidence; it was not a source of drinking water, but a means of washing away the blood of a *hara-kiri* suicide. Today it is known as Okiku's Well.

Okiku was a beautiful woman who worked at the castle and was the favorite servant of a great lord. Her devotion to him ran deep and she harbored a secret desire to be loved by him. Her tragedy began when she overheard one of her lord's chief retainers plotting to overthrow and kill the Lord of Himeji and usurp the castle. Horrified, she revealed the plot to the lord instantly. Although her fast action had saved the lord's life, the chief retainer had escaped and had learned of Okiku's role in averting the assassination. He determined to take his revenge.

Part of Okiku's duties was the care of ten precious plates, a collection particularly treasured by the lord. Beautifully gilded and of incalculable worth, it was a great honor for Okiku to be given the sole care and responsibility for this collection. The retainer managed to steal one of the plates, thereby raising a suspicion that Okiku had stolen it. She was tried for the crime and found guilty. To add to her misery, the lord she had loved and whose life she had saved granted permission for the traitorous retainer to torture Okiku to death in a series of horrific, sexually degrading acts. Finally Okiku's dead body was thrown into the well.

The betrayal, heartbreak, and humiliation of Okiku's death ensured that her soul could find no peaceful repose. Her *yuurei* began to haunt the well into which her mutilated body had been thrown. In the early hours of every morning (the classic time for *yuurei* hauntings is between 2 A.M. and 3 A.M.), her voice would wake the lord from his sleep in the Donjon, as she counted the precious plates from one to nine, breaking into unearthly, ear-piercing screaming and wailing before she reached ten. This nightly torture ultimately resulted in the complete breakdown of the lord's mental health, who had soon discovered Okiku's innocence and knew her death had been wrongful.

The story of Okiku's Well is a key story in Japanese culture, where it is now known as *Banshu Sarayashiki* and has been the subject of many variations in theater and literature. But at Himeji Castle, there are still those who say they have heard Okiku's howls in the still quiet hours of the early morning. The brutality of her murder and the profound sense of betrayal she felt are still so strong that she remains imprisoned by her own earthly emotions, her soul unable to find peace.

Epilogue

Deep into that darkness peering, long I stood there, wondering, fearing,
Doubting, dreaming dreams no mortal ever dared to dream before.

EDGAR ALLAN POE

Now you have peered into that darkness, you have glimpsed neither dreams nor wild imaginings, but true accounts. For those who experienced these encounters first-hand, there can be no room for doubt. Many were left deeply disturbed while others found comfort in the empirical proof of life after death. All were marked by the impact of a foretaste of a world beyond our understanding.

Throughout history, most civilizations have shared a belief in life after death and in ghosts. From the darkest and remotest corners of the globe to the busiest inner city, many people still accept that we are living alongside a spirit world. Ghosts do not just reside in the crumbling castles of literature, or in the macabre graveyards of our nightmares. They are climbing in our mountains, flying in our planes, floating in our ships and seeking refuge in our modern, comfortable homes.

Are these apparitions a part of a science we have yet to understand?

Science admits that it does not have all the answers. Indeed many leading scientists will tell you quite the opposite, acknowledging that it is our vast lack of understanding of the world that drives them in their quest for knowledge.

In the words of Carl Jung,

> . . . A great deal will be discovered which our present limited view would have ruled out as impossible.